Nobody's ever up when I call anymore
I'm always here but there's no knock on the door
Nothin' goin' on after midnight these days
~~They crazy friends & had knew~~
~~the~~ those crazy friends have All changed their ways

(Bridge)
So I sit ~~there~~ underground with a
Bottle ~~and~~ in the smoke
In the cave where I've been
Bound to laugh at my own joke
~~at~~ ~~~~ ~~myself~~
~~~~ The blame is mine they all
tried to find me
The only place they didn't look
is behind me

THE BILLY BOB TAPES

BILLY BOB

THE BILLY BOB TAPES

A Cave Full of Ghosts

THORNTON

with Kinky Friedman

wm

WILLIAM MORROW
An Imprint of HarperCollins*Publishers*

THE BILLY BOB TAPES. Copyright © 2012 by Billy Bob Thornton. All rights reserved. Printed in the United States of America. No part of this book may be used or reproduced in any manner whatsoever without written permission except in the case of brief quotations embodied in critical articles and reviews. For information address HarperCollins Publishers, 10 East 53rd Street, New York, NY 10022.

HarperCollins books may be purchased for educational, business, or sales promotional use. For information please write: Special Markets Department, HarperCollins Publishers, 10 East 53rd Street, New York, NY 10022.

FIRST EDITION

Designed by Jamie Kerner

Library of Congress Cataloging-in-Publication Data has been applied for.

ISBN 978-0-06-210177-8

12 13 14 15 16 OV/RRD 10 9 8 7 6 5 4 3 2 1

This Book is dedicated
to this guy.

And this guy.

You can't get healthy
By taking thirty different
Kinds of pills a day.
On the other hand,
You can't fix a compound
fracture by shaking
a chicken foot at it.

From 'Poor Buds' Almanac'

Billy Bob Thornton

by Angelina Jolie

WHERE TO BEGIN? I FIRST HEARD FROM SHARED FRIENDS THAT THERE was this man who was "like the hillbilly Orson Welles." I couldn't imagine how that description would manifest itself. Then I saw *Sling Blade*.

I sat alone in a theater full of strangers equally engrossed in the film. Every nuance. Every facial gesture. The sound of the chair as it's dragged along the floor. The characters. Each one completely original and yet it's as if you knew them intimately. You watch as the filmmaker helps you to understand a place in time and people who he knows so well. You are getting to know him. His mind. His humanity.

Through the years I've known Billy I've learned that not only was he as interesting, as truly original, as had been told to me, but that he was also so much more. I smile as I write this, as my instinct is to say, simply, he is not a "normal person." But he isn't. I have known him now for more than a decade and I still haven't quite figured him out. Not that I want to. The puzzle is so much fun.

But I know this—

He has an unmatchable wit and can make you laugh until your face hurts.

He has insomnia; he uses it to work obsessively on music until the sun comes up. My favorite recordings are when he tells a story. I like his raw voice with only hints of sounds that illustrate the feeling behind the story. He knows what I mean. "The sound of the rain hitting the tin roof . . ."

He had a talking bird he trained by forcing it to listen to hours of Captain Beefheart. She liked to swear.

He's a bit agoraphobic, and it's really a miracle that he gets out of the house to make films. If he could shoot them in his basement he would.

I threw a surprise party once, ignoring the fact he hates crowds and being social. When they said "Surprise," it was as if he had been stabbed in the gut. He went pale and had to hide in the kitchen.

He did eventually come out.

Billy's mother is psychic, and he worries he, too, has the gift. He can't tell the difference between a dream, a thought, and a dangerous premonition. It's why he has to correct it in his mind. He has to put things back into alignment. To be with him is like being with a mad mathematician. He is constantly counting and repeating.

To him, I am the number four. May sound strange, but it means a lot to me.

We often joke about how much I loved Ed Crane, the character from *The Man Who Wasn't There*. He was beautiful in that. But I also knew things that others didn't notice. I remember there was a courtroom scene, and when the judge would bang the gavel, Billy would squirm. The thing is, it wasn't because of the scene, it was Billy trying to work out his OCD and the judge kept hitting the gavel a different number of times. Sometimes a good number. Sometimes not. And Billy was squirming trying to will him to hit it again.

He hates Komodo dragons, and even reading this he will shiver at the name. There was one incident . . . hard to explain. Can't really.

He watches old sixties TV shows to remember better, simpler times when he feels down. If he's not watching that, he's following baseball.

One of my favorite things is to watch Billy play an entire game of baseball with himself on the tennis court. Only himself. Not easy to do. He throws the ball, calls out the action moment to moment. He catches the ball. Scolds or congratulates his teammates. It's fascinating. Some who don't know him well might call it crazy if they watched it for hours on end. But then, you don't know Billy.

Billy still writes all his songs and film scripts on yellow legal pads. He scribbles on them and often draws pictures of ugly characters doing something ironic. I remember one morning waking up and he had been up all night filling one of those yellow pads with a story. Just one night and it was done. Perfectly done. And then, being Billy, he put it away and didn't write again for years.

I keep trying to convince him to go spend time on a porch in the South and write the Great American Novel. I know it's in him. I hope we get to read it one day. Maybe he's already written it, on one of those yellow pads. And he's put it away somewhere. Somewhere that may never be seen. I wouldn't put it past him.

Most of all, he would die for his family. He has a big beautiful heart.

Some people walk through life able to quiet the voices in their heads. He can't. And I, and everyone else who knows him well, we love him for it. I know one thing: the world would certainly be a hell of a lot more dull if that man weren't in it.

Behind the Scenes

ONE WORKING TITLE FOR WHAT YOU HOLD IN YOUR HANDS WAS *Billy Bob Talks,* and that's literally how the book came into existence. An ever-changing cast of characters assembled by Kinky Friedman gathered at Billy's place night after night, assigned the task of getting him to talk—and keeping him talking—with the tape recorder running. It's not that Billy was reluctant to talk. He wasn't. But it was hard for him, as it would be for anyone, to talk without people listening. As Kinky said of us, Billy's audience, before one of the final sessions, "We're all just furniture."

Some of those gathered weren't content, however, to be simply furniture. Danny Hutton, a founding member of the rock band Three Dog Night, who came to one recording session, matched every one of Billy's stories with one of his own—much to the consternation of Kinky, who was there to get Billy's stories, not Danny's. Billy, a Three Dog Night fan since he was a teenager, didn't mind and saw Danny's visit as an opportunity to play him a few tracks by Billy's own band, the Boxmasters. Billy's politeness wasn't shared by Kinky when it came to Ted Mann, writer for the television shows NYPD Blue and Deadwood and frequent guest during the recording sessions for this book. Kinky had to keep reminding him to "shut the fuck up." Ted's response, using a line cribbed from another attendee: "You're stealing my humanity!" There was general agreement, though, given the stories he told, that a Ted Mann book wouldn't be bad either.

The sessions—recorded by J. D. Andrew, cofounder of the Boxmasters—were fueled by beer, cigarettes, espresso, and, in Kinky's case, cigars, and often ran hours past midnight. One night, Billy slipped into the guise of Karl from *Sling Blade*—voice, facial expression, hand-rubbing, *mm-hmms,* and all—for an improvised monologue about his guests, and then went right back to being Billy to demonstrate that getting into character isn't all that difficult, despite the big deal some actors make about it. Another night, actor J. P. Shellnutt came by with ZZ Top guitarist Billy Gibbons. One of the final recording sessions concluded with Louie Kemp, who put together Bob Dylan's midseventies Rolling Thunder Revue tour, explaining to Billy how Orthodox Jews such as himself prepare food to ensure it's kosher.

Amazingly, even with all the distractions, entertaining though they were, Billy Bob did, in fact, talk, and the book you're reading is the result. Not everything made it into print, though, and a lot of the stories that ended up on the cutting-room floor—including one bawdy tale about Billy's underwear drawer from his teenage years, which he feared would embarrass his mother should it be included here—are as entertaining as what was included. Maybe they'll end up in the sequel. And perhaps that book will get the title that, to the disappointment of some of us "furniture," was ultimately rejected for this volume: *It Only Hurts When I Pee* by Billy Bob Thornton.

—DANIEL TAUB (A FIRSTHAND OBSERVER)

"Why a Book Now?"

A LOT OF PEOPLE HAVE WANTED TO DO A BOOK ON ME OVER THE YEARS. Usually journalist types who wanted some cheap Hollywood biography, where I talk about fighting with an actor on the set, or who had sex with whom, and I would never do that. No one should. But when Kinky said, "Hey, let's do a book with some weird and funny stories about growing up and you can also bitch about whatever's on your mind," I said, "Okay, not such a bad idea."

If I ramble and curse a lot, it's because this book wasn't written, it was recorded, and a lot of it isn't edited. It's just as it came out, so there'll be some of that, so please forgive me.

The other reason I did this book is because I wanted to put my two cents in about how I truly believe our culture is crumbling before our eyes and a lot of people seem to be pretty apathetic about it. I believe that we are in a society that is encouraging, funding, and rewarding laziness, cynicism, mediocrity, and cruelty. And for some reason we've become a society that believes that it is judge and jury. Puritanical when convenient for itself, and just the opposite when that is more convenient.

There is a lot of selfishness, hatred, and self-entitlement going around. And we're being hoodwinked by companies that sell stuff to us because they know our weakness, the need to be accepted and noticed. I believe we need a cultural revolution, and I don't mean simply "It sucks"; I mean "It's an emergency!"

And one real problem is that a lot of people from my generation will play devil's advocate for this horseshit just so they can be part of what's hip and to hang on to their own popularity by selling shit that, at the end of the day, they don't even believe in. These people fought for a certain type of freedom back in the day, and now they are selling it down a muddy river. Freedom does not mean creepy, cowardly, social warfare.

More than ever, art has become a product. And where our souls are concerned, it's really expensive.

Other than that, I guess everything's okay; how 'bout you?

"Cave Full of Ghosts"

Nobody's ever up when I call anymore
I'm always here but there's no knock at my door
Nothin's going on after midnight these days
Those crazy friends have all changed their ways

So I sit here underground
With a bottle in the smoke
In the cave where I've been bound
To laugh at my own joke
The blame is mine
They all tried to find me
The only place they didn't look is behind me

Sometimes I see shapes in the air
Sometimes I see the faces that they wear
Maybe they're old friends that don't mean any harm
Could be the chill I feel is meant to keep me warm
As I man my lonely post in this cave full of ghosts

Sleep won't come but exhaustion never goes
My consciousness is haunted by dreams that never show
My way of life grew up and moved right out of town
And left a body that no one ever found

So I sit here underground

With a bottle in the smoke

In the cave where I've been bound

To laugh at my own joke

The blame is mine

They all tried to find me

The only place they didn't look is behind me

Sometimes I see writing on the wall

Sometimes I hear laughter in the hall

Maybe it's just old friends leavin' me a note

Reminding me the future is something they rewrote

To close the book on a cave full of ghosts

—"Cave Full of Ghosts" (Thornton/Andrew)

CHAPTER ONE

Alpine, Arkansas: God's Country

I'LL GET INTO ALPINE BY TELLING A STORY.

My great-great-great-great-uncle or however many greats he was, was a captain in the Confederate Army. His name was William Langston. I named my son Willie after him. William Langston Thornton. Sounds kind of dignified, right?

William Langston—whose brother James Langston was my however many greats-grandfather—was from Alabama, and he had a sweetheart before he went into the Civil War. They loved each other madly. She was a great gal and wanted nothing more than to marry this man and have a family with him. But William was about to go into the Civil War and he didn't want to marry her, even though she was the love of his life.

"I'm not going to make you a widow," he said, "because I don't know if I'll come out of this thing."

In one of the battles, he was injured. The polite way to say it is that he suffered a war injury that prevented him from having children. The not-so-polite way to say it is he had his nuts shot off. I think maybe the whole rig, you know what I mean? But when he got out of the war and came back home, she still wanted to marry him.

"The most important thing in the world to you, your dream,

was to have children and a farm and raise a family," he said. "I can't do that."

She said, "I don't care, I love you, I want to marry you anyway."

"I'm not going to do that to you," he said, "because you will at some point, someday, meet someone, marry them, and have a family. I'm not going to ruin that for you. I'm not worth being married to because I can't give you a family."

So William left and became a drifter. He drifted through Texas and ended up in this place called the Chalybeate Valley. I'm not sure how the French might pronounce it, but the way they say it in Arkansas is KU-lee-bet.

So William Langston got to the Chalybeate Valley, and he stood on top of this hill that overlooked the valley. That hill is now a roadside park with one or two picnic tables and maybe one of those stone grills where you could barbecue something if you want to. He was looking over the valley there when he wrote a letter to his brother, James Langston.

I've seen God's country, he wrote. *I've seen the most beautiful little valley in the world. I plan on homesteading here and you should come too.* So his brother moved *his* family there, and that valley became Alpine, Arkansas.

When my son was born in 1993, I thought it would be nice to name him after a guy who could never have kids. Here's this name, William Langston, a name that ended there in the Chalybeate Valley, so I named my son William Langston. But one way or the other, that's how my family came about in Alpine, Arkansas.

CHAPTER TWO

Character Study

The friends that came along

Are characters in songs

The tune's not always strong

But the truth's not right or wrong

Nowhere, nowhere

Gave me a home for free

Somewhere, somewhere

Is always calling me

—"Somewhere" (Thornton/Andrew)

I NEVER SET OUT TO BE LIKE SOMEBODY. THAT'S NOT TO SAY THAT INFLU-
ences don't creep in over the years. You watch things, you love people, you have heroes, and you get influenced eventually. I was obsessed with short stories and Southern novelists like John Faulkner, William Faulkner, Erskine Caldwell, Flannery O'Connor, that kind of stuff. But from the time I was born until now, my writing process has always been about my observations and experiences.

As a little kid, as young as three maybe, I was already inter-ested in characters, and Alpine was *rich* with characters. They were just everywhere. Like the ones that would come into our house to get their taxes done by my grandmother, most of them loggers who hauled billets or worked at the sawmill in Glenwood for a living.

And we loved stories. We'd sit on the porch and listen to our grandmother and grandfather or some old man from down the road visiting. Visiting was a big thing. See, the South is just different from other places. The air is heavier, for one, but you can feel the ghosts there. There's something about the fact that a war was fought on our own soil, in Vicksburg and places like that. With African-Americans, there's this long history about the spirituals. What they used to call Negro spirituals all came out of the Africans coming here as slaves and working in the fields. Those songs and later the blues came out of those fields. Similarly, I think for the sharecroppers and the white folk around there, country music actually came from the old men who'd sit on Coke crates out in front of the store or on the screened-in porches or in the yard under the hickory nut tree, spinning yarns and just talking about people who lived there. See, these stories didn't have to be made up. The characters were already there, so the stories just came out of the characters we knew. I really believe that that rich sort of hillbilly culture is where country music came from and why some guys like me ended up writing and telling stories or becoming actors or musicians. Country music, real country music, is just different from other types of music. The songs are usually driven by stories. I mean, if you hear Merle Haggard do "If We Make It Through December," it might be just three minutes long but you get it.

But from the time I was three years old, I was aware of people and interested in characters and the weird shit that went on around me. And I came from this little bitty place being influenced by a mini–literary society within my family. My mother, Virginia Roberta Faulkner, was an English major, and my dad, Billy Ray, was a history teacher and a coach. My grandmother was a schoolteacher and a writer. My uncle Don was a musician and singer. Years later I was the drummer for his band. This was old-fashioned country shit. We played VFW clubs, stuff like that. That's why I get pissed off when people say, "Oh, he's an actor trying to be a musician." It's like, I've been playing at VFW halls since I was a fucking teenager.

But anyway, we lived in a little town called Alpine; there were about one hundred ten people living in this valley. There wasn't much to it. There was one store that was called Carmie Buck's Grocery that had a post office and a gas pump, and that's all there was. We lived with my maternal grandmother and grandfather, and we were raised the Indian way. There were Cherokees and Choctaws on my mom's side of the family, and there was some Italian in the mix, too. We were Choctaw on her dad's side, and when my grandmother would get mad at my grandfather, she would call him "an old gut-eating Choctaw." We even had some burial mounds on our land, and if we played on them we got our asses beat for it.

Our family had a well, a little old garden, and a bunch of dogs and cats, but we didn't really raise cattle and all that. They didn't have any running water or electricity until I was probably nine maybe, and when it gets dark out there, if you don't have any electricity, it gets *pitch*-dark. So up into the midsixties, they literally read by coal oil lamp and went to sleep at seven, like Abraham Lincoln.

My grandfather was a medic in World War I. I used to put his gas mask and helmet on and run around, and he would whip my ass for it. When he retired he became a forestry man, working for the Forestry Service, and part of his job was to climb the tower a couple of times a day, take his binoculars, and look around to see if there were any fires.

You could see all the way into Oklahoma from the top of his mountain. He would give me his binoculars and say, "See those mountains over there? Way back there? Those are in Oklahoma." That was crazy shit to me when I was a kid, climbing that tower and looking at a mountain in Oklahoma.

My dad's family was raised around a place called Glenwood, Arkansas, which was about twenty or thirty miles away from Alpine. Glenwood's a town of probably one or two thousand people, so to us, being from a town with a population of one hundred ten, *that* was a city. Where I was raised, if you went from Alpine to Glenwood, it may only have been thirty miles but you might as well have been going to Vienna. It was a huge trip to go pretty much anywhere. I didn't know anything about travel growing up. Shit, I never flew on an airplane until my twenties, so to me, if you went to Little Rock, you went to the moon.

My grandfather was like Daniel Boone. He hunted and we ate squirrel like people eat chicken. Like today, one guy might ask, "What are you going to eat today?" The other guy might say, "I don't know, grill some chicken." That's the way we were with squirrels. By the time I was six or seven years old, I was shooting the eyes out of squirrels, skinning them and cleaning them so we could have them for supper. Here in my house in the middle of L.A., we've got some of the biggest, fattest fucking squirrels I've ever seen in my life. I go out on my balcony to have a smoke and I see like twelve squirrels running around the yard that are plump little shits. And I have to admit that even though I am practically a vegan these days, I *still* imagine myself up there on my balcony with a .22 rifle, picking off those fat little shits and bringing them in, skinning them, and frying them. Squirrels just have a special taste to them. It's like the old saying goes: you can take the boy out of the hills, but you can't take the hills out of the boy.

My family was sort of the literate people around there. My grandmother, Maude Faulkner, was a teacher in a one-room school. She wrote magazine articles, poems, and even a novel that was never published. Some of it was lost, or I would get it published now.

Because there was a lot of illiteracy around there, she also did everybody's taxes. But people wouldn't really pay her money most of the time, because they didn't have any, so they would pay her in trade, with a quilt or a pot of beans, maybe a bushel of corn. A friend of mine once said, "I remember when I was growing up, everything was fried in Crisco." I replied, "Shit, we had Snowdrift," which was the *off-brand*. So, I guess we were pretty poor, but we were poor people in a place that was really fucking poor. *I* never thought we were poor. We weren't starving. We ate all the time. I mean, I didn't really eat store-bought meat until I was in the first grade. If you live in the country, there's always something to eat. And it wasn't just squirrels either. My grandfather killed other shit, too—possums, turtles, raccoons, everything.

CHAPTER THREE

It's Real Hard to Get Away with Shit

Look at all the thoughts we hide
If anybody likes you it's gotta mean you lied
Our tongues are tied

—"American Jail" (Thornton/Andrew)

WE MOVED INTO A TOWN CALLED HATFIELD WHEN I WAS IN THE first grade. I'll never forget that place. It had about twenty thousand people in it. One of the churches, Presbyterian I think, had lost their preacher, and so they let my dad—who was a basketball coach and a history teacher—and our family live in the parsonage. That parsonage was probably the best house we ever lived in.

A lot of shit happened there in Hatfield, a lot of crazy shit—at least to *me* it was crazy shit. It's like every time I hear somebody reminiscing, "My grandmother, I'll never forget, made the best biscuits," I'm like, "Who fucking cares? So did mine. *Everybody's* did." But when you're a kid, everything looks bigger than it really is.

My grandfather, I don't remember why, came and stayed with us for several weeks one time. He was this old crusty guy, as I said, like Daniel Boone. He didn't say much, but when he said something, it usually meant a lot.

When I was a kid, I always wanted everybody to like me so much that I would just do any fucking thing I was told. Like if somebody were to say, "Hey, let's go steal that truck and drive to Little Rock," I would say, "Oh, okay, but do you like me?" and if he said, "Yeah, I like you, sure, let's go," I'd be in the fucking truck with him. That's a hypothetical situation, but when I was in the first grade, I had a buddy in the second grade who would talk me into shit all the time.

One time he said, "Tell your grandpa to give us fifty cents for some cigarettes," because he wanted to smoke. This would be my first cigarette, but I guess he had smoked before because he already had this shit figured out. The way it was back then, you could buy a pack of candy cigarettes that looked just like the real thing. They looked like a pack of Pall Malls or Chesterfields or whatever it was, but they'd use a slightly different spelling, like "Chesterfeel." And they had two different kinds. One was this long chalky candy, and that you would just eat. The other actually had paper around it with a filter and the candy was in the middle. If you blew, the powdery shit that was on the candy became a little puff of smoke. That's the kind my buddy said we should get.

So we went to my grandfather and said, "Hey, can I have fifty cents?" My grandfather asked us what we needed fifty cents for, and here's how stupid I was: I didn't think to just say we wanted to go buy some candy. I said we wanted to go buy some candy *cigarettes*.

Now, my grandfather was a smart old son-of-a-bitch. Not only had he been through World War I, but he was a good hunter, and good hunters are real smart usually. He gave us the fifty cents and said, "Don't go getting into any damn trouble," but what he meant was, "I'm going to let them learn a lesson." I guess he was figuring we would go get cigarettes and just get sick and puke.

Back then, in a little town, especially in the South, you didn't have to be eighteen or twenty-one to buy cigarettes. You could send an infant in there if you wanted to get a pack of cigarettes—because your parents always sent you somewhere to get shit. I used to go get Kotex for my mother when I was thirteen, you know?

So we went down to the store, and I said, "My dad wants a pack of cigarettes." The guy said, "What kind do you want?" I said, "Winstons."

A shed full of wood and straw and paper goods is probably not the best place to smoke your first cigarette. Long story short, we burned down the shed and the volunteer fire department showed up. My buddy and I went out on the porch and watched it burn with the whole family. My grandfather whispered to me, "Did you go buy your candy cigarettes?"

"Yes, sir."

"Did you burn that shed down?"

I didn't respond.

He just kept looking at me. After a while, I realized what he was saying to me without actually saying it was, "I'm not going to tell anybody, but it's real hard to get away with shit. So don't fuck around."

Now, when I look at my own daughter Bella, who's seven, I can't imagine her doing anything except looking at her dinosaur books and playing around the house. But I burned down a shed in the first grade.

CHAPTER FOUR

My Mom and the Gift

Hey there Mama, am I ever gonna feel good again?
Can you hear me every night when I call your name?
I hope you can.

—"Am I Ever Going Home Again"
(Thornton/Andrew)

MY WRITING PARTNER TOM EPPERSON AND I WROTE A MOVIE CALLED *The Gift,* which was made with Cate Blanchett. It's based on my mom, who is a psychic. Of course, the studio wanted to turn it into more of a thriller kind of film, and the finished movie didn't end up exactly the way it was written.

My mom didn't talk about being a psychic when I was growing up. Me and my brothers didn't even know what a psychic was. But she took appointments, and we had a coffee table with magazines on it just like at a doctor's office. In the back, in my mom and dad's bedroom, there was a room we called the Blue Room because it had blue curtains and a blue wall. I'd get in from school and there would be three or four women sitting in our living room. My mother had a few male clients, but she saw mostly women because men back there, they're a little more closed off to things like that.

There was a guy that came to our house one night, a businessman who was a big redneck in town. I was maybe twelve or thirteen. We were all asleep. My dad wasn't there—he was working the graveyard shift at a cable plant—so I went to the door when I heard the knocking. I opened the door, and this guy was standing in a white buttoned-down shirt and holding this troll doll—the ones little girls used to play with. He asked, "Is your mother home?" I said, "Yeah," and went back and got my mother.

"Mom, there's some guy at the door wants to talk to you," I said, and when she saw who it was, my mother told me and my brother to go back over around the corner in the hallway, where we listened to the whole thing.

He started yelling, "If you don't stop seeing my wife and my daughter, then I'm going to start using your own medicine on you. You see this?" he said, holding up that troll doll. "This is a voodoo doll, and I'm going to use it on you if you don't quit talking to my wife and daughter."

He's been dead forever—ended up having a heart attack while he was sleeping with some chick is what I heard—but my mom's still traumatized, it shook her up so bad. To this day, she says she has images of him and thinks it's him every time a doorbell rings.

We got a lot of threats and hate mail. My brothers and I were also teased at school about my mom being a psychic. One time I was walking home from school with a bunch of other kids—we didn't hang out with them, they were walking down the same street we were—and they pointed at our house and said, "There's that house where that old witch lives." That was the first but not the only time we heard someone call our mother a witch. I put my memory of that experience in *The Gift*.

My mom doesn't read for people anymore—just a select few who have been her friends for years—but she was kind of a renowned psychic. Still is. The police used to ask her to help them. So would politicians and all kinds of wealthy people. They'd fly in from New York or Memphis. But my mom was not only a *psychic*—people liked her because she'd also talk and listen to them.

CHAPTER FIVE

Don't Ever Call Him Daddy

We all go through the portal
Yeah, no one's immortal
But the time and the place puzzle me
I'm a prisoner of the details
My theory always fails
To free me from death's mystery

—"They All Fall Apart" (Thornton/Andrew/Davis)

MY PARENTS, BROTHERS, AND I WOULD MOVE TO DIFFERENT TOWNS, but my dad was kind of hotheaded, so he'd lose jobs and we always ended up coming back out to my grandmother's place in Alpine. He had a bad temper and would tell somebody to kiss his ass just like that. He worked as a car salesman sometimes, but he was mainly a teacher and a basketball coach. Small-town basketball team, that was everything where I was from. Imagine a more intense version of *Hoosiers,* that was kind of like my dad's bag.

My mom said my dad was crazy about me until I started talking. After that, he didn't seem to like me that much. He liked my brother Jimmy. He didn't have much time to decide if he liked my brother John or not. John was about five or six when my dad died, so he was more like a son to me and Jimmy. I was twelve when John was born, Jimmy was ten. We kind of raised him after our dad died. My mom was having readings there at the house and we were watching John.

John was very quiet as a kid. He grew up and joined the Army, where he became a medic, and when he got out, he went to the University of Louisville. He went through part of medical school, but then he had a family and started having to make a living. He couldn't really afford medical school anymore, so since then he's been an RN. He's been teaching nursing, which I think is a great thing for him. He's one of the few people in the medical profession that I can actually stand, other than Richard Dwyer, a doctor who saved my life, but I'll get into that later. John's a very smart guy who knows about every fucking disease on the planet, so what I try to do is never talk about that shit with him because if I have one conversation with him about medicine and the new germs and shit they're finding, in my mind, I'll have everything in the world. I'm a little like Woody Allen's characters, like a neurotic Jewish guy from New York. I'm a hypochondriac and everything else.

Anyway, my dad used to whip the shit out of me with a belt, and he hit me a couple of times, too, with his fist. But when I was sixteen, I hit him back. Then it pretty much stopped.

When I was fourteen, my dad got a job at a cable plant, so we were able to move into a three-bedroom brick house. That was the American dream where I came from. But when I was seventeen, right after I graduated from high school, he was diagnosed with lung cancer, that type that you get from asbestos—and he died eight months later. He was forty-six, I think.

My dad never stayed in a hospital. After he got sick, Jimmy

and I shared a bedroom, my mom and my little brother shared another bedroom, and we had my dad in this other room. He was only in the hospital when he went to get cobalt treatments and shit like that, so over a period of eight months I got to see firsthand what it looks like to have your parent die right in front of you. Where they deteriorate into nothing and don't look like themselves, you know what I mean?

Until he got sick, my dad was pretty healthy. He was only five-eight, five-nine, but he was a tough little son-of-a-bitch. He was a boxer in the Navy. I never looked like him or anything. He had real light-colored hair and blue eyes. Somebody told me one time that all the Old West outlaws, 80 percent of them or something, had blue eyes. Very few gunslingers and outlaws had dark eyes unless they were Mexicans or Indians.

A lot of people to this day want me to hate my father, and I never did. I never liked him, but I didn't hate him. I loved my father, he was my dad. We never had a conversation that I remember. I remember just little pieces of things where he actually did something with me. Like, he would take me and my brothers to see the blue herons during the time of year they were flying through this marshy, swampy area out in this field.

My dad was a little bit like the Great Santini. He just loved football and thought I had to be a football player or I was an idiot. He would throw a baseball around with me a little bit and come to my games, even though he always thought baseball players were pussies. He'd say, "You piano players and baseball players are all a bunch of queers." I could live with that. But if I lost one of his tools, I was fucked.

In his defense, his dad was like that, too, all those guys back then were. Willie, my son, will have seven of his friends over here at one time playing video games and hanging out on the porch.

Coming down the stairs, I'll see some kid I've never seen in my life at my refrigerator and I just let him do it—I'm nice to them and all—but when I was growing up, you'd go over to your friend's house and you *prayed* that their dad never saw you. You'd go hide in another fucking room. I was scared of everybody's dad, and to this day I have a problem with older men. Robert Duvall is like my mentor, and I desperately want him to like me, but at the same time I'm scared to death of him.

But when my dad was dying, that was it. I saw him deteriorate into this little bitty skinny bald-headed guy that weighed eighty pounds or whatever, and I still looked at this mean motherfucker as some kind of hero, because he played football, because he was a coach, because he was my dad.

I used to carry him, get him under the knees and under the arms and literally carry him to the table to eat, because he didn't want to eat in the bed. He looked like somebody out of Auschwitz if you saw him, but he still wanted to do things like a regular person. I can remember many times carrying him to the table, and we would crumble up corn bread that my mother made for him in a glass of buttermilk—it's a Southern delicacy—and he'd eat it with a spoon. But he would take two or three bites, puke all over the table, and I would carry him back to his room.

I guess when the cancer gets in your brain you start thinking all kinds of crazy shit because he started to think he had spiders and snakes on him all the time. He would yell in this weird voice that didn't even sound like him, and I would have to go in there and pretend I was getting the spiders and snakes off of him. But once I said I got them all off, he was pretty satisfied.

He also started admitting all this shit to me, but I don't think he knew he was doing it. One time he went, "Don't ever call him Daddy." And I said, "Who?" And he said, "That man your mama's going to marry, don't ever call him Daddy." I said, "All right, I won't." Sure enough, she married this man and I never called him a fucking thing.

I didn't cry until years after my dad died. I forgave him for all the shit because now, looking back, I understand all that he went through. He was a guy who couldn't articulate things, and he was trapped inside a head that he felt like he was *more* than. I forgive him for everything, and I love him, these days, because I saw his fire and his passion, about sports, at least I always thought he was all right.

CHAPTER SIX

Uncle Don and Them

M Y MOTHER'S BROTHER BO WAS IN THE BATTLE OF THE BULGE IN
World War II. We had all this military history around the
house. That was real big back then because before rock and roll,
soldiers—the boys returning home—were actually like rock-
and-roll stars. Of course, when Vietnam came along they were
treated like dirtbags on the corner begging money from people,
which is unfortunate.

The first time I ever had a drink of beer was with Uncle Don
and Uncle Roy when I was about five. Those were the days when
you had to have a church key to open the cans, so Uncle Roy took
out his church key, and they opened up their beers and poured
them into their jelly jars. It was like whatever jelly you had, when
it was gone, you just washed out the jars and those became your
drinking glasses. Uncle Don had his Jax beer, and my uncle Roy
was drinking his Schlitz. It was the best-looking shit I ever saw
in my life. It looked like apple juice.

I asked my uncle Roy what beer tasted like, and sure enough
he said, "Tastes like apple juice, you want a drink?" If I told
anyone now that I gave my five-year-old a drink of beer, I'd be
in jail. Anyway, Uncle Roy said, "You want a drink?" and I said,

"Yeah." Of course, I nearly puked because I expected apple juice and I got that bitter beer taste.

But Uncle Don was my hero. He was like a god to me. In reality, he was an alcoholic who got into knife fights, but to me, he was just this cool guy. Later on, when I was in my twenties, I got compared to him a lot, which was good to me and maybe bad to some other people. Uncle Don was a country musician. Sang like Jim Reeves and played the guitar left-handed, upside down, like Jimi Hendrix. He looked kind of like Errol Flynn, dark, with a little mustache. He was in the Army in the Korean War.

Uncle Don taught me about music and he taught me about life. He was the most charming son-of-a-bitch in the world. He was married like six times or something, and he always married chicks who could play bass.

Uncle Don and his friends stayed drunk a good deal of the time. They'd drink the vanilla flavoring, the cough syrup, whatever was in my grandmother's cabinet. One of his friends drove around in a brand-new truck with no passenger door on it. The passenger door was missing because, after they lost their jobs, they took the door off and sold it to a parts place in Hot Springs to get money to buy liquor.

Uncle Don had a friend from down the road who drank some canned heat or kerosene—I can't remember which—and he died from it. I'll never forget when that happened. They came running out of the house—my grandmother, all of them—and went running down the road because somebody found the guy swollen up and dead out in a field.

I remember another time being on the porch—we had a screened-in porch, as most people did back then, with a swing on it—as a little bitty kid, two or three years old, and watching my uncle Don in a knife fight with a guy in the front yard, which was mostly dirt, because it was just a road that came up to the front door. My grandmother was in the middle of them, screaming, "Please, Don, don't do this!" and Don screamed back, "Mama, get out of this, you don't need to be out here!"

At some point during all the commotion, he accidentally cut her hand real bad. She came back into the house crying and saying, "Yeah, he's cut me." Everybody gathered around her, putting bandages on her hand while Don was still out there in the knife fight. But then I remember him coming in, and just the look on his face from having cut his mother . . . I'll never forget that look that he had.

Don was a carpenter by trade, but when he would lose his carpenter job, he would come back and stay with my grandmother, too. So, just so we're clear, there were times when in one house we had my dad, me, my brother Jimmy, who was two years younger than me—my youngest brother, John, was born years later; my grandfather, who was up on the tower looking for fires and killing shit; my grandmother, who was doing people's taxes; my uncle Don and one of his wives; a few cousins; and my mother, who would see images in the well. That was what my house was like as a kid.

CHAPTER SEVEN

Testifying Turkey Ass and Pawn Shop Prosthetics

KARL FROM *Sling Blade* WAS PARTIALLY INSPIRED BY ALPINE CHARAC-
ters. As I said, there were a lot of characters there.

Then there was my grandma's friend, this old lady who would write little articles for the paper in Arkadelphia. Arkadelphia is the town closest to Alpine, and when I was a kid it was home to about ten thousand people. We would go into town one Saturday a month to get supplies or whatever, and ultimately I would go to college there at Henderson State University, where my parents had both gone. Anyway, one time there was a dispute over some property issue where some guy was mad at another guy because the guy put his fence row too close to his place, or something. So the guy who was mad about the fence decided to take matters into his own hands. The guy with the fence raised chickens and turkeys and had some prize turkey he was fattening up for something, so the first guy sodomized the other guy's turkey and killed it. I don't know if he choked it while he did that, I don't know if he killed it just by screwing it, I don't know, but one way or the other, the first guy fucked the other guy's turkey to death, and they went to court over it.

This friend of my grandmother's came running up to my grandmother's house, saying, "Maude, you never gonna believe this! They've saved that old turkey's butt for a witness!" Now what it really was, to my understanding, is that they froze it or put it up in bags so they could examine the anus to get the guy's stuff, or whatever, as *evidence*. But she said *witness*. So my mother always said she had this image in her head of this turkey's ass on a witness stand testifying.

My cousin Mark was this brilliant hyperactive kid who mostly hung out with my brother Jimmy. Mark was inventive and real crafty. His head ran faster than most people's, but he just couldn't control himself and always found himself in some kind of mess.

He ended up having a motorcycle wreck and lost a leg. One time, Mark came into my aunt and uncle's, and he didn't have his leg. He had gone down and pawned his artificial leg to a pawn shop. My mom said, "I understand Mark pawning his leg because he does stuff like that. What I *don't* understand is what the pawn shop owner wants with an artificial leg."

Mark is the guy who introduced me to this sort of semi-retarded guy or whatever he was, who lived in town up in Arkadelphia. Every town's got a guy who's what they used to call shell-shocked. Now there's some other term for it. Post-traumatic stress disorder. Used to be shell-shocked. Anyway, this guy could have been one of those, but there was something wrong with him, maybe it was like autism. We didn't know about autism or anything like that in those days. Regardless, we used to pick on him some, because kids do shit like that—you know, pick on the retarded guy. He wasn't a kid, he was an older guy.

Now, when I say older guy, when I was a kid, somebody forty was an old man to me. My dad died when he was forty-four or forty-six, I can't remember which, and I thought he was an old man. In any case, kids can be pretty cruel.

Anyway, this guy would just kind of mumble and shuffle around town, and he had a root that he could hang out the side of his overalls, where they dip down by your hip. He could *pee* outside his overalls. He used to chase us sometimes because we fucked with him, but if any of us had any loose change we would pay him to pee outside of his overalls because this son-of-a-bitch, he had a fucking joint on him, it didn't even look human. It literally looked like it came from an animal—like a mule dick or something. I don't remember *exactly* what it looked like, I didn't look that close, but it was a hunk. Anyway, we would give him dimes and quarters, shit we were going to buy Twinkies with but instead pay this guy to pee out the side of his overalls.

THERE WAS THIS ONE FAMILY MY MOM KNEW BACK THERE IN ALPINE. The old man worked in the logging woods while his wife, like a lot of women at the time, would birth kids and work to the bone keeping the house, working in the field, working in the garden, that kind of stuff. She was twenty-nine or thirty but looked real old.

A lot of guys were jealous and would keep their wives away from everything, but this particular guy was so jealous, when he would go to work in the logging woods, he would board his wife up. His kids would go to school, and he would nail two-by-fours over the doors so she couldn't get out while he was gone.

Years later, when they started getting more modern things, his wife got a douche bag—I guess she'd been to a doctor and he said, "You should use this douche"—but the old man cut it to pieces with scissors and threw it out in the yard. He didn't want her putting *anything* in her. "You're not using shit like that," he said—because I guess a douche bag has got a little nozzle on it, stick it in your whatever. But anyhow, he would board her up while he was at work.

The kids would go to Carmie's store after school, and they would ask if Carmie—who was a real nice old guy—had seen their daddy so they could get in the house, but the daddy would be hiding behind the freezer with ice cream. Carmie told us about this. Their daddy would buy ice cream, and he would hide behind the meat freezer while he wouldn't let his kids eat anything but mustard and biscuits. That's what he sent them to school with, and that's where I got the thing with Karl in *Sling Blade* where he eats mustard and biscuits.

When kids used to go to school back in Alpine—this was in my mom's time, not mine—they would take their lunch to school in a lard bucket. Only we called it the dinner bucket, because in the South we didn't have lunch. We had breakfast, we had dinner at noon, and we had supper. So we never heard of lunch. Anyway, kids would take a *dinner* bucket of biscuits because we ate whatever was cheapest. And if you're at school all day, butter and mayonnaise would spoil, so my grandmother used to put mustard on the biscuits because mustard wouldn't spoil quick. But a lot of kids would *only* have biscuits. There was a lot of beauty in Alpine, but there was also a lot of poverty.

So the jealous guy's kids would just get to eat beans, corn bread, stuff like that. They never got anything from the store that would be considered a luxury, like bologna or anything from the meat counter.

But the dad would go buy an ice cream at the store and hide

behind the freezer if his kids came into the store looking for him. He would tell Carmie to tell his kids he hadn't seen their daddy because he didn't want the kids to see him back there eating an ice cream.

People like that. That makes you want to write shit. Tom and I wrote a screenplay called *The Sounds of Country,* which I'll probably never make because I don't want to make it for Hollywood. I'd rather just be satisfied knowing I wrote the story of my uncle Don. Anyway, when I tell people some of these things, they look at me like I'm from another planet, but I lived in this.

"THE TOM EPPERSON STORY" BY TOM EPPERSON
(AS TOLD TO TOM EPPERSON)

Part I

I was born in 1951 in the little southwest Arkansas town of Nashville. My family moved to the somewhat larger town of Malvern a year later, and that's where I grew up. My father was a lawyer and judge. My mother, like virtually all mothers in those days, was a housewife. I had three sisters.

I was a bashful little boy who hated school and didn't make very good grades. I loved to read comic books (we called them funny books) and to fish on Lake Catherine and to go to the Ritz Theatre and see neat movies like *Attack of the Crab Monsters* and *The Creeping Unknown.*

When I was twelve, the Epperson family got some new neighbors. The Thorntons. Billy Bob was eight. He wore glasses and had buckteeth and looked remarkably like the Ernie Douglas character in *My Three Sons* (and he actually was one of three sons). We had some things in common—we both liked sports and monster movies and funny books—but a four-year age difference is a vast chasm when you're a kid, and I certainly didn't regard him as an equal. When my friends and I needed a body to round out the sides when we were playing basketball or touch football in the backyard, Billy Bob was brought in.

We had a nickname for Billy Bob. "Silly Slob." We played mean tricks on him. Once when Chuck Shryock and I attempted to retrieve an errantly tossed football from some bushes, we encountered a yellow-jacket nest and were driven away. We were standing around trying to figure out how to get the ball out of there, when who should come walking down the sidewalk but little Billy Bob. We told him we couldn't get our football out of the bushes because we were "too big" to get in there. Billy, always eager to be included by the big kids, was happy to help us out. He crawled back into the bushes, and then an instant later tore out of there with the football under his arm, screaming as yellow jackets swarmed around him and stung him repeatedly. Chuck and I laughed our heads off.

CHAPTER EIGHT

"Dangerous News in Safe Town"

Safe town, safe town
The shiny surface binds
Dig down underground
What do you think we'll find?

—"Dangerous News in Safe Town"
(Thornton/Andrew)

WE MOVED TO A LITTLE TOWN OUTSIDE OF ELDORADO DOWN IN THE southern part of Arkansas. There was a paper mill there that made the whole town smell like shit all the time. One of my memories of that place happened during the time when my brother and I had mono, which we got real young—I was in the second grade and he wasn't even in school. There was a big storm coming, and it was just pissing down rain. The lightning was the kind that lights up the whole fucking world and you can see everything at midnight. Something happened outside the house, and my dad went to check on it. There were all kinds of people milling around our front yard, and I'll never forget going out on the porch in my Roy Rogers pajamas, me and my brother Jimmy. We weren't supposed to go out there, but when you're a kid you're curious. It's like, "Daddy went out in the front yard, what's going on?"

We lived right next door to the elementary school, and there was a ditch out by our front yard in the road there. A guy had gotten hit by a car, and it killed him—cut his head half in two, and he was lying over in the ditch. We couldn't see him very well because it was pouring rain, but it happened so close to our house that people were walking across our yard to get a better look.

Jimmy and I were standing out there in the rain in our pajamas watching this when some guy walked by and said, "Aw hell, it's just some nigger." When people heard that comment, all of a sudden they weren't really interested anymore. That was the first time I realized, wow, some people don't think black people are as important as white people.

We didn't have black people in Alpine. We didn't know anything about black people or segregation until we moved from there. Up until I was twelve or so, we had separate drinking fountains in public places, and when you went to the doctor's office it had different entrances—a regular entrance for white people, then on the other side of the building you had COLORED ONLY.

After that, we moved to Malvern. It's about forty miles from Little Rock, which is about an hour and a half from Memphis. My dad got a job coaching at a little school called Rural Dale, in the town of Lonsdale, which was right outside of Malvern. This was in 1963, so I would've been in the third grade when we moved there. I thought it was funny that the school was called "Rural Dale" but the town was called "Lonsdale." I always wondered how it went down during the school-naming meeting:

What should we call our school?

Fuck, I don't know.

Hey, our town is called "Lonsdale," so why don't we name the school "Rural Dale"!

Yeah!

Rural Dale it is. Meeting adjourned.

Malvern had a population of about ten thousand people, so to us that was like going to Paris. It was one of those typical Southern towns—in fact, it's actually the town I wanted to base *Jayne Mansfield's Car* on. The town we shot in, Cedartown, Georgia, is very much like Malvern was. For a town that size, Malvern had a crazy number of bands, which was great for me, because I loved music, even at that age. I met my writing partner, Tom Epperson, in Malvern. He was our neighbor.

I saw segregation in Malvern and that separation of races was most noticeable to me at the Ritz, our one movie theater in town. I loved movies, and I would go to the Ritz Theatre as often as I could. Sometimes they'd have a food drive for "the needy"—that's what they called the poor then—and you could see a movie for bringing canned goods and nonperishable food. In those days, on Saturdays, they would almost always show a double feature, so you could go and see a movie, stay and see a second movie, and they didn't kick you out. You didn't even have to pay to stay and see the double feature *again* if you wanted to. We would stay all fucking day Saturday and Saturday night if it was something we wanted to see. We'd sometimes see a double feature three times in one day.

When you went to the Ritz Theatre, the white people came in through the front by the popcorn stand and the black people went in another entrance in the alley that had a staircase going into the balcony. When you watched a movie, there was this whole white audience downstairs and this whole black audience upstairs. And black people were very vocal—*especially* in horror movies. White people didn't say much, but black people were like, "Girl, you better not go in that basement, he's gonna kill you like he killed that other girl!" You'd hear all that extra commentary going on up in the balcony during movies. So our experience with black people, up until they integrated the schools, was pretty much when we would hear them talking up there in the balcony.

The thing is, when you're a kid, you don't know all this shit. You don't understand that Doctor So-and-So is having an affair with the real estate agent's wife or any of the other goings-on in town. You think all adults are responsible people who take care of shit while the kids just run around. It seemed weird to me that black people and white people were separated, but as a little kid, you didn't sit around and dissect all this. You just lived your life and did your thing, and I was a kid doing my thing. I liked everybody.

"THE TOM EPPERSON STORY" BY TOM EPPERSON
(AS TOLD TO TOM EPPERSON)

Part II

Growing up in Arkansas in the fifties was not unlike growing up in apartheid-era South Africa. The racism against black people was out in the open. It was proud and it was smug and it was ugly and it was defiant. It dared you to say something different. I knew from an early age that it was wrong, but nobody around me (and I mean not one person) seemed to agree with me, and I learned then a very important lesson: never take anybody's word for anything. A single person can be right, and a whole society can be wrong. Indeed, society is probably usually wrong.

CHAPTER NINE

"In the Day"

Do you remember in the day

All our crazy summer ways

And those guys that were our friends?

The red and yellow windy falls

When we seemed to have it all

And it was never gonna end

The girls we loved that came and went

All the idle time we spent

Playing records that we'd borrowed

Now it kinda hurts to think

Every time I take a drink

That this would be tomorrow

—"In the Day" (Thornton/Davis)

STARTING IN JUNIOR HIGH SCHOOL, A LOT OF MY FRIENDS WERE BLACK. I was fucked with at school about hanging out with them, but music is where I connected with the black kids. I was in a band that formed from a band called Blue and the Blue Velvets, which was all black except for me. It was a band called Hot 'Lanta, which was about half and half. Actually, all through high school—up until I was about twenty—I played in either all-black or part-black bands.

We lived near downtown, in the white part of town, which was just a main street with a Western Auto, an Otasco, and a Ben Franklin. Unlike the black neighborhoods, the white neighborhoods weren't named. You just lived out on Highway 9 or you lived "in town"—unless you were a doctor or a dentist or something like that. Then you'd live with your family in our one rich neighborhood, Reedwood. You might look at one of these Reedwood houses today and say, "I could set that goddamn house in my kitchen," but back then we thought the houses in Reedwood were fucking mansions.

I tried to get every Reedwood chick I could. For some reason rich chicks always liked me. I guess to them I seemed like some kind of rebellious, edgy guy. I was an innocent kid in a lot of ways, but I was also the kid who got into fights.

We were poor people who lived pretty close to the tracks in Malvern, near the black neighborhoods. There was West End, East End, a neighborhood called Cross the Creek, and Perla, which was out by the brick plant. I fell in with this group of black cats who lived in East End, which I'm going to write a movie about one of these days.

East End was the heavy-ass neighborhood. That's where you went if you wanted pretty much anything. There was even a bootlegger there, a big black woman who shall remain nameless. When it was cold, we'd warm our hands by a fifty-gallon drum with a fire in it. Kind of like the doo-wop guys would do in New York City. The sign that someone was a bootlegger was that they had a pop machine on their front porch. And by bootlegger, I don't mean moonshine. Moonshiners lived outside of town. Bootleggers were people who sold beer, whiskey, and wine, but they sold it for twice the price it would cost at a liquor store.

We lived in a dry county, so the bootlegger was for people who didn't want to drive to fucking Hot Springs a half an hour away and get in a drunken head-on collision on the way home.

Hot Springs, where I was actually born, is a resort town—sort of the Miami of Arkansas. It has a colorful history: Jesse James hid out there; Al Capone had a house there. There were a lot of Jewish people, too. They even had a couple of synagogues. We had one Jewish family in Malvern, but we didn't know they were Jewish, we just thought they had a weird last name.

I was playing in a band with black cats who mostly lived in East End. Now, the difference between a white band and a black band, at least in my town back then, was, if you were a white band, your biggest trouble was if the parents of one of the guys in the band had some other shit they wanted them to do that night, like go to the Old West dinner theater in Little Rock to see a play or something. Even if the gig was scheduled and you were about to get in the car to drive to Batesville or Fort Smith or Memphis or wherever, then you didn't have a guitar player that night. The biggest problem with a black band was, when you were supposed to get together and rehearse, usually at one of the guys' houses or out at the barbershop—there was this old black man in East End who owned a barbershop and would let us rehearse in there sometimes—you could never find any of them. Like, even if the last time you saw them you said, "All right, Wednesday night at eight," and they said, "All right, man, see you then." Without fail, I would wind up in my '67 Buick Wildcat with bucket seats and a factory eight-track tape player, driving all over the fucking town trying to round these guys up.

I'd try the barbershop, and they wouldn't be there. Then I'd go to one guy's house and his wife would say, "I think he's over in West End." Then I'd get back in the car and drive over to West End, check around, and they would say, "I think him and a couple of guys were going over to Hot Springs." It wasn't beyond me to drive to Hot Springs to look for them.

You have to understand, all I wanted to do was play music or listen to it, one or the other. I couldn't wait. That was the highlight of my day, every day. I even went to pick up one of the guys one night and he was in a fight with his wife, and she shot at him with a .22 pistol and hit the couch about a foot from where I was sitting. He and I ran out the front door and hid down a bank across the railroad tracks. I said, "Do you think we can make it to the car?" which was between us and the house. And he said, "We better not. She'll cool down in a little bit. Besides that, my bass is in the house."

From the ditch we watched her go back inside the house. We waited around and waited around until she finally came out and started cussing at him. He kind of came up from behind the tracks and started yelling back. They cussed back and forth a little bit until, finally, he went up there. They talked calmly on the porch and then went inside. He came out after a little bit with his bass, like nothing happened. We got in the car and left.

Now, in itself that may not be that interesting a story, but this kind of thing happened all the time. Not the getting shot at part, necessarily, but it was never "we're going to rehearse at eight" and everybody would be there.

Nevertheless, they were the most interesting, fun, talented sons-of-bitches I ever met, but they were the kind of guys who were scared to leave home. There are people in little towns in this country who are so much more talented than any of the people we hear playing in bands today, but they grew up the old-fashioned way. They're terrified to leave their little town. You get a job over at the ball bearing plant and you know you better keep it.

CHAPTER TEN

"Saturday Afternoon a Half a Century On"

. . . Paula's record shop, with rows of records waitin'
For dreamers to flip through them one by one
Hey, there's one we just saw, on Bandstand *they were ratin'*
Just look at all those labels, like Roulette and Sun.

Saturday afternoon a half a century on
Bewildered ghosts line all that's left of Main Street
The magic left with the digital dawn
The remnants pass as whispers in retreat.

Yeah, I'm gonna have the nerve to say
That those were the days
And I'll say it right in your face
Yeah, I'm gonna have the nerve to tell
A story that's hard to sell
To the Bank of Wireless Wizards and their fools
That bought this place

—"Saturday Afternoon a Half a Century On"

(Thornton/Andrew)

THE TIME I REMEMBER THE MOST IN MALVERN WAS MY LIFE IN MUSIC, because that's all I wanted to do. I grew up hearing my uncle sing songs by Jim Reeves, Hank Williams, Webb Pierce, Jimmie Rodgers. That kind of country music was really my first music; we didn't know anything about the blues.

And then Elvis came along.

When we finally got electricity at my grandmother's house, we got a radio, and that's how I heard Elvis Presley. Elvis really did something to me. I heard his songs on the radio, and I thought, *Wow, that's amazing*. These days it's real easy to think that Elvis Presley was just this fluffy kind of deal, but when he came along, he changed things. Elvis didn't write songs, so he wasn't a songwriter. He was just this big star and he was sexy. A lot of people don't really know who Elvis's real influence was, but I do because I'm close to a lot of people who were close to him because I grew up near Memphis. They tell me that who he really wanted to be like was Dean Martin. People always say that Elvis's big influence were the black gospel singers, and he did love that stuff. But if you listen to Elvis sing, and then you listen to Dean Martin sing, you'll notice that. Listen to "Everybody Loves Somebody Sometime." You'll get it.

My uncle gave me a little Roy Rogers guitar that had a picture of Roy Rogers and a little rope on it. I would bang around on that. One Christmas somebody gave me one of those little washtub things made out of tin that looked like one of those pedestals in the circus, that the elephant puts his foot up on. In fact, it *did* have some kind of circus shit on it; it was pink and blue with a picture of elephants on it. It was one of those things you could stand on and pretend you're in the circus. The first song I ever wrote was called "Cat Shit on a Rat Box." That was the only line, and I even remember the melody, it kind of sounds like a Chuck Berry song. I would stand on that elephant stand and bang that song out on my little Roy Rogers guitar, over and over and over.

In 1964 the shit hit the fan in music. My brother Jimmy and I were instantly rock-and-roll junkies, and when we saw the Beatles on Ed Sullivan, *that's* what changed my life; you try to tell a kid nowadays what it was like to see, with your own eyes, history being made—most of them don't get it. My son Willie gets it, which is great. I can tell him about it and he'll listen to it. By the time he and his brother, Harry, were seven and eight, I turned them on to Mothers of Invention, Captain Beefheart, and the Bonzo Dog Band and all these people. I think that's why they "get it."

Anyway, I remember when Jimmy and I first saw the Beatles on our old black-and-white Zenith TV. We were literally lying on our stomachs on the hardwood floor, looking like something out of a Norman Rockwell painting, watching the fucking Beatles when they first came to America. I'll never forget that shit as long as I live. They did "She Loves You," "I Wanna Hold Your Hand"—they were such heroes. When I saw them that day, I knew *that* was what I wanted to do. When the Beatles came along, their sound actually changed the world. I mean, even though they were playing their pop songs at that time, it changed the world. Their sound was completely different—they were influenced by skiffle music they had in England, along with listening to Chuck Berry and Carl Perkins, which is ironic because here, nobody gave a shit about Little Richard or whoever until the Beatles. The British Invasion was good for this reason. English bands who grew up listening to American music on the radio would listen to all this wild shit and they would take a Chuck Berry song, or a Little Richard or Carl Perkins song, or whoever it was, and they'd play it in a way that was palatable and acceptable to the people in America on the radio. But the way they played, it didn't sound like Chuck Berry. It sounded like *them* doing that. So the way that sounded was just this perfect mixture of things that created what we know as sort of pop-rock music. It was an amazing deal.

So then, of course, every night Ed Sullivan was on, my brother and I were in front of the TV. We saw the Animals, the Kinks, the Stones, Freddy and the Dreamers, Billy J. Kramer and the Dakotas, Peter and Gordon, Chad and Jeremy, all of them, and that became my obsession. We started our first band with no instruments. We used cardboard boxes for drums and we sang with a pretend microphone, a mop or whatever it was. We took rubber bands and stretched them over cigar boxes. The Dave Clark Five was one of our personal favorites, so the first songs we probably ever played as a band were on cardboard boxes doing "Glad All Over" and "Catch Us If You Can."

I got my first drum kit when I was nine. It was from a Sears or Montgomery Ward catalog. It was this little kid set with cardboard heads that I broke real quick. Later, when I finally got a real set, it had Mylar heads. I thought Mylar sounded pretty fancy, like something Dave Clark played on. Of course I broke those in half pretty soon too.

When I was thirteen or fourteen, there was a kid named Don who had a red sparkle Ludwig drum set—"kit" didn't come along till later, they called it a drum "set" when I was growing up. Don and I played against each other in Little League—we were both pitchers—and I used to go hang out by his house to watch him play left-handed drums with his band, and I would be eyeing that red sparkle Ludwig drum set.

I *begged* my parents, and I had to work it off, but they paid

$150 for this used Ludwig red sparkle drum set without a high hat—just one cymbal and four drums. I've got a picture of that somewhere.

MY FIRST REAL BAND WAS CALLED THE MCCOVEYS BECAUSE IT SOUNDED like the McCoys. The McCoys were a band from Union City, Indiana. They did "Hang on Sloopy," which hit number one on the Billboard charts in 1965. Their guitar player was Rick Derringer, who later on became a big guy with Johnny Winter. In those days we had one amplifier and you plugged two guitars into it, each in a different channel. We had no bass player. I played drums. We played instrumentals because we didn't have any microphones. We loved the Ventures so we would do "Walk, Don't Run," "House of the Rising Sun," and "Hanky Panky" by Tommy James and the Shondells. We did an *instrumental* version of "Ballad of the Green Beret" by Sgt. Barry Sadler. The whole point of the song is the guy doesn't sing, he talks. And it's a story about this guy talking about *"fighting soldiers from the sky, fearless men who jump and die"* . . . See what I mean? So it's kind of pointless to do the song without the words. It's like "let's do an instrumental version of *Cat on a Hot Tin Roof.*"

The big band in my town was called the Yardleys. The British Invasion was in full swing at the time, and they named themselves the Yardleys because it sounded British, like Yardley of London that made all the perfume and scented soap. The Yardleys were Steve Walker, Larry Byrd, Bo Jones, Bucky Griggs, and Butch Allen. They had a Farfisa organ, bass, guitar, drums, and Bo Jones played the trumpet. They played original songs and actually made a couple of 45s that were played regionally, but they may as well have been the fucking Rolling Stones or the Beatles as far as I was concerned.

The Yardleys used to have these street dances, and they would rope off the main Dollar Store and Safeway parking lots. It cost fifty cents or a dollar to come inside the rope and dance in front of the band. Me and my buddies, we were just little kids who wanted to be in a band. We only wanted to hear the music. We were like "Fuck, we don't have fifty cents to pay just to step like two feet from here and get inside the rope." I used to just stand out on the sidewalk outside the ropes, listening and watching every move they made.

I was so mesmerized by these guys. I was in this little band that nobody gave a shit about until later, and the Yardleys were these older, sophisticated guys—seniors, when I was in junior high. Most of my days in junior high and high school were spent trying to figure out how you get chicks that looked good, and just standing there watching these bands like the Cadets, LSD and the Illusions, the Senates, the Yardleys, and the Beethovens.

Later on, this band called Brass Button came along. These were guys in my class and they became the big band in town. They were a horn band. They did Chicago; Blood, Sweat, and Tears; and all that stuff. I was always real jealous of them because they were *the* big thing in town and it was harder because they were my age. It wasn't like The Yardleys, who were years older than me. It was like "GODDAMMIT! These guys!" Rick Dial was in the Brass Button; he's an old friend of mine who passed away recently. He was in *Sling Blade*; he played the heavyset guy who ran the Fix-It shop. He was going to be in *Jayne Mansfield's Car,* too.

My brother started a band and then I had my band. My brother and I never played in a band together. The guys in his band were a couple of years younger than us so we always had this competition. Their band really hated our band so we never played together. My brother and I used to fight all the time. I loved this kid, but we still fought.

Bucky Griggs was the drummer with the Yardleys. Bucky had glasses that came way down on his nose that he kind of peered out through. He had this real hot girlfriend named Joan. She was beautiful. Her little brother was a friend of mine, so I used to go over and sneak around his house just to look at her.

I remember when I was twelve years old, going to a Yardleys dance at the old gym, which was just a concrete floor. Joan came over and said, "Do you want to dance?" I started shaking like a leaf and sweating and shit. I was like, "No, that's okay." But she got me by the hand and pulled me onto the dance floor in front of the Yardleys. I never moved because I didn't know how to dance, I still don't. I always thought people dancing looked stupid, especially from up there onstage where you can see them making faces or whatever. Anyway, I stood there sweating while she danced around me.

Speaking of hot girls, I have to mention a girl named Donna. She was a senior when I was in the ninth grade, and to this day I still think about her. She was like a cheerleader or something. Pep club gal. She wore an ankle bracelet. You could put an ankle bracelet on a kangaroo and I would hit on it. There was just something about those ankle bracelets that always did something to me. But I never said a word to her. When I'd see her, I'd just start sweating. She was my big crush all through school, and I've never spoken to her once, to this day.

Just as memorable as the night Joan made me dance with her was when the Yardleys were playing a cover of "Cold Sweat" by James Brown. Steve Walker, the guitar player, landed on a nail on the wooden stage during his guitar solo. When he got back up, his pants were ripped and he had this bloody knee but he kept playing. I was like *Yeah! This is what I want to do one day! I want to cut my fucking leg open and play rock and roll!*

Whenever the Yardleys would rehearse at Bo Jones's house, I would go with a couple of buddies and we would hide in the hedges outside the living room and listen. Bo Jones lived in a three-bedroom brick house, which was the ultimate thing you could have back where I came from.

When the Yardleys would see us standing out there in the hedges, they would usually chase us off. But one day Bucky Griggs came out on the porch and said, "How come y'all always hanging around out here?"

"We just want to hear y'all play," I said.

"Y'all want to play in a band?"

"Yeah."

"What do you play?"

"I play drums."

"You want to come in and look at my drums?"

"Yeah."

But like I said, to me, at that time, it was like Ringo Starr just said, "Hey, you wanna come on in and play my drums?" I guarantee it was every bit that big in my mind. Bucky had a pristine red sparkle Ludwig kit with Zildjian cymbals. It was amazing.

"You can sit down and play them if you want to," Bucky said. I couldn't play much at that point. I could play stuff like "Hanky Panky" by Tommy James, or "House of the Rising Sun," shit like that, but I didn't want to embarrass myself in front of Bucky, so I just sat down, took the sticks, timidly tapped each drum a little bit, tapped a cymbal real light. He goes, "No, go ahead, you can play them," and I mumbled, "Nah, that's okay, thank you," and I got up and hauled ass out of there. That was my brush with the Yardleys.

In Malvern we had one record store in town. It was called Paula's Record Shop. Paula was an older lady even back then when I was in junior high school. She was a little gruff and bossy, but she was great. She really loved her little record shop. My brother Jimmy and I used to go in there all the time, and we usually didn't have the money to get anything, but once in a blue moon when we did we would go inside and buy something. I think a 45 was fifty cents and a record album, in the early to mid-sixties, was probably anywhere from $1.99 to $3.99. We couldn't wait to get in there and just thumb through all the records. Some of the 45s had a white paper sleeve and you could see the label through it, and others would have a full picture on the sleeve. I remember a few of the Beatles 45s had a full sleeve with a picture on it. We would stare at the pictures and read what liner notes we could without opening the record up, which we couldn't do, obviously. We'd read the back and look at anything that was on there. Sometimes you would see something that would just strike your fancy and you didn't know why. It was magical.

Paula also had a small selection of instruments, and I remember I bought my first tambourine in there. She had a couple of guitars, like Teiscos or something like that, not real expensive ones, and there was usually at least one drum set available. Sometimes she would just have a snare drum with a cymbal on it. Sets like that used to be popular back then. They were very simple—a snare drum on a tall stand and a little cymbal stand attached to the snare drum. I can remember guys playing drums that way; I did myself for a little bit.

Jimmy and I were in there when we saw the first Black Oak Arkansas album. We didn't know who Black Oak Arkansas was. This would have been in 1970, I guess. The band was just these long-haired guys standing on an old flatbed truck. One of the guys was lean, and he had long blond hair and a walking cane. That was Jim Dandy. We thought, *Wow, Black Oak Arkansas,* which is a real town in Arkansas, they had named their band after their town. They grew up around there, not too far from Memphis, so they had that sound. When we finally got the money we bought that record, and we were just blown away. If you haven't heard that first Black Oak Arkansas album, you must. I highly recommend it. Jim Dandy had that gravelly voice, and they were all great musicians. Their songs were unique, unlike anything we'd heard before. Most people know them from "Jim Dandy to the Rescue," but that first album, with "Uncle Lijiah," "Hot and Nasty," and "When Electricity Came to Arkansas," was just incredible. Years later I was playing in a band called Nothin' Doin' with Mike and Nick Shipp, two brothers from Benton, Arkansas (where we later filmed *Sling Blade*), and we got to know the guys in Black Oak Arkansas very well. We ended up opening for them a couple of times. They were always real good to us.

About three years ago, the Boxmasters were playing a show in Memphis and Jim Dandy actually came and sat in with us. Jerry Lee Lewis and Mickey Gilley were there too. It was pretty amazing.

Paula's Record Shop is also where my brother and I first saw all these records by the Mothers of Invention. Here, we saw these weird ugly fucks on the covers of these records (and by Zappa's own account they were ugly motherfuckers, so that's not me saying it). Jimmy Carl Black, Roy Estrada, Frank Zappa, Lowell George were in the band at one point, but those early Mothers records, with Ian Underwood, Billy Mundi, all these guys, we just loved their stuff. I remember the first Mothers album I bought was probably *We're Only in It for the Money*. From the time Jimmy and I were little kids, 1966, 1967, we were in love with the Mothers of Invention and everything about Zappa. Frank died before I could meet him, but I became friends with Moon Zappa, Frank's daughter, and to this day I'm very good friends with the Zappa family, and to me it's just such a huge deal because it changed my life, hearing the Mothers of Invention. Later on we heard Captain Beefheart, the Bonzo Dog Doo-Dah Band, music that people considered at the time avant-garde. That really changed me and Jimmy. We branched out.

Jimmy started learning to play the guitar and he got very good at it. He played banjo, guitar, piano—just about everything. I learned guitar well enough to write songs on it. When I was in junior high school, I got to go to my first real concert, which was a band called Ides of March. They did that song "Vehicle." And then my first *huge* concert right after that was Three Dog Night. I was in a thing in the Methodist Church, the MYF group, the Methodist Youth Fellowship, and they would take us on field trips. They took us to see Three Dog Night at Barton Coliseum in Little Rock. I thought, *Geez, maybe one of these days, we'll get to open for somebody that big.* A lot of times my brother and I couldn't afford tickets, but that was one thing my mom was real good about. She made sure we had enough money to go to concerts. She just wouldn't tell my dad.

By the time I was in high school, I was at Barton Coliseum every time someone was there, so I got to see Ten Years After, Emerson Lake and Palmer, the Allman Brothers, and Creedence

Clearwater Revival in their heyday. Creedence Clearwater Revival was the best show I think I ever saw in my life. The opening act was Freddie King, a great bluesman from Texas, who did "I'm Going Down." He was fucking amazing. I got there early. We always tried to get to the coliseum really early so we could be right by the stage and that night, I was right in front. I was wearing these judge's robes I had taken from the theater department at school and I was a little high. Freddie King just came in there and blew everybody away. There were three acts: Freddie King was the first act and the second act was Tony Joe White, with that song "Polk Salad Annie." He was fucking amazing. Then Creedence came out. Nobody went onstage and said, "Ladies and gentlemen, Creedence Clearwater Revival!" They didn't have to. *That* was the mark of a legendary band already in their own time. The lights went down in the coliseum, everybody went nuts, and you saw the bluish-purple lights on those Kustom amplifiers. It was so dark that I could just barely see the figure of John Fogerty right in front of me. Then the lights went on at the instant he hit the opening chord for "Green River." I'm just standing right there and there's fucking John Fogerty wearing a western suit looking down at me. I was just like "Goddammit!" These days, you go to a concert and you see a marble floor and people out there with no fucking amplifiers and no stacks of speakers and shit, it's just like an empty stage with dancers. That's no good. That's not a concert; that's a fucking television show.

Our influences were everything from the Mothers of Invention and Captain Beefheart to Alice Cooper, the Allman Brothers, Marshall Tucker, Wet Willie, Grinderswitch, all the Southern rock stuff, to Tom Jones and, of course, the British Invasion. I was never big on Motown because I was a Memphis guy—Malvern is only a couple hours away from Memphis so I was raised around that Memphis sound, like the Boxtops and the Buckinghams. I was a big Isaac Hayes fan. I liked the Temptations pretty well, but I loved Stax Records. That was the heavier shit, and so I was into all that. Blue and the Blue Velvets, the band I wrote about earlier, played some great soul shit, that early seventies soul like "Everybody Plays the Fool" and "Me and Mrs. Jones" by Billy Paul. Also during that time there was Al Green, the Isley Brothers, and then you had the horn bands like Con Funk Shun and Brass Construction—it was just a great time in music. When I was in Hot 'Lanta, we did a lot of rock-and-roll versions of soul songs. We'd take a soul song and do a rock-and-roll version, and we'd take a rock-and-roll song and do a soul version so they kind of met in the middle. We sounded like a soul/rock group.

In 1974, we went to Muscle Shoals, Alabama, and we made a record (actually, it wasn't a record, it was a reel-to-reel tape). For $250 we went to Muscle Shoals and recorded at Widget Sound in Sheffield, Alabama (Muscle Shoals and Sheffield were all there together). Back then, the Muscle Shoals sound was considered the shit, and I got to record in one of those studios where the real shit was recorded back then, where Otis Redding, Aretha Franklin, and all those people recorded. I'm friends now with a lot of those guys, like Donnie Fritts, who was one of the original Muscle Shoals Sound guys. He wrote a lot of songs; he was one of those original Muscle Shoals writers. He wrote "We Had It All." I also know Jimmy Johnson and all the guys in the Muscle Shoals rhythm section. Barry Beckett, who was the original organ player, played on my first two solo records that were on a real label.

This whole era was incredible. I was playing with Hot 'Lanta and a band called Nothin' Doin' (which I had tattooed on my arm). Nothin' Doin' was just a full-on rock-and-roll band. It was three guys: me and two brothers from out of Benton, Arkansas, Mike Shipp and Nick Shipp. We played mostly original music, but we would do early ZZ Top stuff. We started getting opportunities—we opened for Hank Williams Jr., Black Oak Arkansas, and Humble Pie. Nothin' Doin' was regionally popular and we played all over the place. Eventually a guy saw us in Houston and came backstage. We were playing in a big rock club there called Cardi's. He was a guy who had worked for the ZZ Top organization. He said, "You guys sound a lot like ZZ Top." I was the drummer at that point. I had been the singer but we couldn't keep a drummer so I finally just said "oh, fuck it" and I started playing drums again. This guy kept saying, "You sound so much like ZZ Top." We would play some of their songs, but we mainly played originals. This guy asked us, "How would you like to do a ZZ Top tribute act?" This was way before tribute acts were a big deal.

"We don't know," we said. "What's in it for us?"

"How much do you guys make in a night?"

"Maybe a couple hundred bucks."

"How would you like to make fifteen hundred dollars a night?"

"Shit yes!"

His name was Scott Weiss and he had worked for Lone Wolf Productions, which was ZZ Top's thing, and now he had his own agency called Electric Artists. Scott put us on the road. I'll never forget this guy. He really was great to us. These days something like that might be considered cheesy, but in those days it wasn't.

We started playing as Tres Hombres and we did this ZZ Top tribute act. We played all over and it was great. We got to open for a lot of big people, and we also did our own shows. It was a fantastic thing.

Over the years, I kind of came up in the music business. I worked as a roadie for a sound company out of Little Rock. They had an agency, too. I had the opportunity to work on shows with the Nitty Gritty Dirt Band, Pure Prairie League, Lighthouse, The Ozark Mountain Daredevils, and on and on. All these bands back in the day. I was only into rock and roll early on, and it wasn't until I was in my late teens that I started appreciating country music. I just thought country music was like this old three-chord stuff that my uncle did. All of a sudden I started realizing the genius of George Jones and Merle Haggard and all those guys. I got into real hard-core country, like Del Reeves, who is a particular favorite of ours. Our band, the Boxmasters, ended up cutting one of his songs, and we're influenced quite a bit by that sound. The musical influences all thrown together, they form you for later on. You might not necessarily hear the Mothers of Invention in the Boxmasters music, other than maybe some of the humor, but little bits and pieces creep in there.

We created the Boxmasters out of our love of sixties music. The name "Boxmasters" sounds kind of like a sixties band, but the direct translation of the word is hard to say on a talk show. Our logo design looks like it's from the sixties, and we decided to order some suits from Liverpool so when we play on the stage, we wear actual Beatles suits and Beatles boots. On our first record we made up this whole phony history about how the Boxmasters came from Bellflower, California (a town that's just car lots, basically). The way we really got together happened while I was working on *Beautiful Door,* my last solo album over at Universal. I met J. D. Andrew. He was working as an assistant to Jim Mitchell, helping me finish up that album. Jim Mitchell is a great friend of ours. He engineered all four of my solo albums and a couple of movie scores.

Jim got a job that was too good to pass up—working at Fox Sports doing the music that they do for the football games. He wasn't available much so J.D., as his assistant, was in here a lot, helping me finish *Beautiful Door.* One night a guy had asked me to do a version of a Hank Williams song for a Canadian television show and so I asked J.D., "You said you play guitar, right?" He said, "Yeah, I play a little bit." I said, "Can you play well enough to do a Hank Williams song with me?" He and I recorded "Lost Highway" by Hank Williams. The song had this vibe that was like the old sixties country music and the British Invasion all in one. I said, "How much do you know about the British Invasion?" He said, "Not much."

The first song I played for J.D. was "Yesterday's Gone" by Chad and Jeremy. I said, "Let's record this and see what happens" and we did. I said, "I like this. All the guys I play with in my solo band, they all live everywhere, all around the country. Do you know anybody locally?" He knew this guy Mike Butler, who's a terrific guitar player. He came over and we formed the Boxmasters. Brad Davis, a great bluegrass player who played in my solo band, he plays with us now. Brad and I have been playing together for thirteen or fourteen years. The Boxmasters are me, J.D., and Brad. We make the records, the three of us. When we tour, there's six of us in the band.

The Boxmasters started out as a thing that was a combination of hillbilly music and the British Invasion. I'm not talking about country music like they have now, but actual hillbilly music and country music of the fifties and sixties. Webb Pierce, Del Reeves, guys like that who we really loved. J. D. Andrew and I put this band together to mix that music with the music of the Animals, the Beatles, and the Kinks, with the Rolling Stones thrown in for good measure. The sound has kind of grown to where we want it to be, which is more just like a sixties rock-and-roll band, without so much hillbilly in it. We first signed with Vanguard, which is an old-school label, and because it *was* an old-school label, they let us use their original label on our records. For our first two albums, we put a bonus CD in there of covers that all the Boxmasters fans love to hear us do live. We ended up doing three albums for Vanguard and we had a great time there. Except for the bonus covers, we did all original music. I've probably written close to a thousand songs. The Boxmasters now have about eight or nine records in the can. Our next one comes out this year (2012).

Geoff Emerick, who was an engineer for the Beatles, said one of the things he loves about our band is that we have a backbeat you can hear. That was a great compliment. We have a great fan base. There's not many of them, but our fans really love us, and we sell enough to keep afloat. If we had come along in 1967, we would have done pretty well I think. Some people are really going to take exception to me saying that, but I don't give a shit because I believe that 100 percent. If we had come along in the mid- to late sixties, we would have been a big band. But it doesn't work that way anymore. We write a lot of good songs, and frankly, we're a pretty damn good band.

A couple of years ago, for old times' sake, I called Larry Byrd, one of the Yardleys, and I flew him out to play organ on the Boxmasters' record *Holy Toledo* with J.D., Danny Baker, and myself. Generally, the guys in the Yardleys wouldn't talk to me when I was growing up, but they were my heroes, and Larry was always kind of nice to me.

CHAPTER ELEVEN

"Providence"

It seems like happiness ignores all navigation

Sometimes freedom comes when you have lost your way

I changed the course of my imagination

And took a turn that leads to come what may

I don't know where I'm gonna go

Right now that's about the only thing I know

—"Providence" (Thornton/Andrew)

I DIDN'T GROW UP WANTING TO BE AN ACTOR OR DIRECTOR BECAUSE WE didn't have that many movies where I grew up. We had one movie theater where I would go and see Don Knotts in *The Reluctant Astronaut,* but that's all I knew about.

I did my first play when I was in the third grade. Our class did "The Three Billy Goats Gruff." If you remember, it was a kids' story about three billy goats that were trying to cross a bridge where a troll lived, but the troll wouldn't let them cross because it was *his* bridge. I played the middle billy goat in that. It wasn't anything big—it was just a little classroom play—and after it was over, I never thought about it anymore.

When I was in the fourth grade, I was a shepherd in the school

Christmas play, and that was the first play I did in front of an audience. It was my first big role. I wore a burlap bag they had made into my costume, and I had some kind of a stick for a staff. The first word I ever uttered onstage in front of an audience in a play was "Hark." That was my one line. After I delivered my one line, another shepherd was supposed to say something, and then the guy playing Jesus got all the rest of the lines. On my cue, I stepped out with my staff and my burlap clothing and I said, "Harp." I had this one-word line, and I said it wrong. Instead of "Hark," I said, "Harp."

I was really shy in large groups of people. I was convinced that everyone else's family had more money and that my peers had more acclaim than I did. I wasn't the captain of the football team or the president of the student council, I wasn't any of that shit. I was just this bucktoothed hillbilly kid that lived in town and was never picked out for anything. Later, I started playing baseball, and I was successful at that so I became more popular among some people, but most of my friends were rejects like me. We had guys in my high school who were really outgoing. Guys who would get up in front of class and sing a Perry Como song. I would always sit in the very back of the classroom.

My parents were both college graduates—my dad was a teacher, my mom was an English major—and I was a dumb ass. I had a learning disability that I didn't even know about at the time. I'm severely dyslexic and can barely read. I also had what they now call ADD, I guess, because I don't retain what I *can* read. But I just wasn't generally interested in school, except for history. I thought history was a subject that was worthwhile. I never understood quite why math and algebra and all that shit was important, unless you wanted to be an algebra teacher.

One time I said to my Algebra II teacher, "I don't understand a subject where they give you the answer and you got to
figure out how you get the question. That doesn't make any
sense to me. I know how you add one and two, I understand
that. But how do you add an x to a y? It's like saying, how do
you add a cow to a tomato?" She told me, "What if you want
to be a building engineer one day?" I said, "Ma'am, I promise
you, I swear to you on my life that I'm not going to want to be
a building engineer." As far as I was concerned, I was going to
be in a rock-and-roll band or pitch for the St. Louis Cardinals.
Those were the only things I had any interest in. But she never
did like me, she was always mean to me. I think the real reason
she didn't like me was because one time I was wearing some
double-knit pants, as we did in those days, and there was this
girl in our class who was amazing. She was like Elke Sommer. I
was at my desk and she was at the board, working out a problem. She had this little skirt on, and it kind of went up when
she would reach up there. I got a hard-on in my double-knit
pants, and then I was called to the board and it wouldn't go
down. It was kind of like something out of *Porky's*. So I went
to the board and I just stood out there, like a whole tent in
my double-knit pants, because they had a lot of room in them.
I didn't ask for this thing to do that. It's later, when you get
older, *then* you start asking it to do that. But back then, at that
time, I did not ask to get up in front of the algebra class with a
tent in my double-knit pants.

After that incident, that algebra teacher just really wouldn't
tolerate me, but I passed that class somehow, with Ds. Maybe
she just wanted to get me out of the school, I don't know.

Needless to say, I made shitty grades in everything. When
I saw that you could take drama class, I thought, *This will be*

great. There will be chicks in there, and maybe I can even get
a good grade because how hard can it be to get up and be the
scarecrow in some fucking play?

The woman who taught my drama class, and this is a name I'm happy to mention, was a woman named Maudie Treadway. Mrs. Treadway wanted people to be who they were and not just sit there with their thumbs up their asses. When I started this class, I didn't know anything about drama, so I would sit there and write short stories and things like that. The class would be doing a scene on the stage, and I would sit there in the back of the classroom alone and write on my own.

One day I was writing a play about a bored guy and his wife in a Kmart. We didn't have a Kmart in our town, and going twenty miles away to Kmart in Hot Springs was a big deal. I wrote this story about Kmart with all this funny dark shit, and Mrs. Treadway came back and got on my ass about not paying any attention to what was going on onstage.

"If you don't want to be in this class, you don't have to be," she said in her booming voice. (Mrs. Treadway was a big woman, with a big voice.) "What are you doing back here anyway? Doodling?"

"No, I was writing this story," I said.

"Oh, really? Let me have it."

She took my notebook away from me, and I thought it was going to be one of those "if it's so important why don't you share it with the rest of the class" kind of things, but it wasn't. She kept it, and the next day she came up to me and said, "I read your story and it was brilliant, I love it. How would you like to do that onstage?" This high school drama class, in Arkansas in 1972, wasn't exactly the center of the theater world. The curriculum was fairly standard. We had the different textbooks where we'd learn about who all the playwrights were, and at the end of the year the class would put on the senior play, which was always some kind of goofy shit, and then that was it.

All of a sudden, Mrs. Treadway was doing something that was unheard of. She was asking a student to do his own original story that he had written in the back of the class and play the character. High school drama teachers didn't do that in Arkansas in 1972, but Mrs. Treadway did, for me. Everything I've accomplished since, I can trace back to this woman, Maudie Treadway.

Mrs. Treadway cast a girl from the class, and this girl and I did the story I wrote, which was about a bored husband and wife going through Kmart. I figured Mrs. Treadway must have liked how it turned out, because after that she started letting me direct my own scenes in class.

One day she kept me after class and said, "I've been teaching high school drama for a living for a long time. You don't know what it's like to be a drama teacher in a small town in Arkansas where nobody really cares, but let me tell you right now . . ."—and I was sixteen years old when she said this, and this is an example of how acting teachers can be helpful—she said, "Let me tell you something right now. You can do this. I've never had a student in one of my classes I actually thought was a real actor. You are. And you're a writer. You ought to try to do this one of these days."

Later, I starred in my senior play. I originally took drama class because there were girls in there and I thought it would be an easy A, but it turns out I liked it and I was good at it.

Mrs. Treadway died not too long after I graduated from high school. I was a pallbearer at her funeral.

CHAPTER TWELVE

My Unremarkable College Career

Imagination climbing up the walls
Remembering a little of my fall
Reality feels liquid in my hands
Thoughts take off in flight but never land
Memories for me just come and go
It seems that I recall a brilliant show
Striking swirling colors that I used to know
Now are just a dull nerve-wracking glow

—"Psychedelic" (Thornton/Andrew)

I WENT TO HENDERSON STATE COLLEGE. IT WASN'T AN EXPENSIVE COL-lege, but it was a good college. It was the same place my mom and dad went to. My mom ended up being an English major there when it was called Henderson State Teachers College. In 1967 it became Henderson State College, then in 1975 they changed the name to Henderson State University. A lot of people from my town went there. My niece, my brother Jimmy's daughter, went there, and she told me they have a plaque at the college that has my name on it, about fulfilling your dreams and how you can be whatever you want to be. That's kind of ironic considering I never graduated because I was too drunk most of the time. But it's a cool, creative school. If you went to Henderson, it meant that you were the real deal. Not in academic terms, necessarily, but it meant that you were a hippie or you were a football player or you had some edge to you.

I mostly hung out with the music majors. I didn't really want to hang out with the jocks, even though I had played baseball in high school. I was never the jock type, like the kind of guy you see in a sports bar. I was the long-haired hippie guy who happened to play ball pretty well. Those music guys were the perfect people for me to hang out with because we all had the same ideas. Some of them were a little squirrelly, but a lot of them had bands that I played with off and on. Some of the first sound jobs I worked when I was a roadie were at the gymnasium at the college. And they didn't have shit bands play there, either. They had bands like the Nitty Gritty Dirt Band. I remember Blood, Sweat, and Tears playing there, too.

In the nineties and up until a few years ago, I always had an easier time hanging out with musicians, until I got my first major record deal. Since then, I've found it easier to hang out with actors. Much easier. It's them being pricks because they don't want me to make records. Mick Jagger is one of the more iconic guys that I used to hang out with a bit—he's a fucking Rolling Stone and he doesn't care about actors being musicians. If I sold ten million records, he'd be all for it. There are a few good ones who are all for me. Levon Helm is all for me. Warren Haynes is all for me. Rickey Medlocke, the guys from Skynyrd, ZZ Top, Billy Gibbons, and Dusty and Frank, they're all old friends and real terrific to me. But I'll never get a Grammy, I'll promise you that. I'll *guarantee* you that. Not that I want one. I'd probably melt it down and fix my fucking carburetor with it.

Anyway, Henderson State was a great college, but if we're being real honest, I pissed my opportunity away. Besides playing music from time to time, I didn't do much of anything there but fuck, drink, and shoot pool over at the Minute Man. I think I only had two classes that I actually earned grades in—Psychology and Western Civilization. The rest of them were incompletes. That was in a year and a half—three semesters if you're keeping score.

When I was at Henderson, I messed around with this chick and got into some trouble with her boyfriend, who was on the football team. He used to chase me around the campus all the time, so I spent most of my college days outrunning that son-of-a-bitch. I'd see him on campus and I'd haul ass. He finally caught me in the room where the mailboxes were. I thought, *This is it, he's going to beat my head into one of these mailboxes.*

"Hey, man," he said, "you can stop running from me. I broke up with that girl. Sorry I've been chasing you all this time, but I was real pissed off at you then. Now I see how she is."

One day a friend of mine said, "Let's go to the Minute Man and shoot pool and eat those forty-five-cent sandwiches from the menu because we can't do anything else." I had no money. The first semester I was there, I was living with my aunt and uncle who used to live in that town. I slept in this extra room of theirs. So my buddy and I went to the Minute Man, and he said, "You're just a dumb ass like me. Let's pledge a fraternity."

"A fraternity?" I said. "Are you high? Look at us. Aren't those like Joe College guys?" He goes, "Fuck no, there's all kinds of people. There's this one fraternity here, they got a house on this street over here. They're the ones always having parties and fun. Let's go to one of their parties!"

So we went to a party, and the guys in the fraternity turned out to be pretty cool. It was rush week, and they talked me into being a pledge. I said to my friend, "What does that mean? What do I have to do?" And he said, "You stay drunk all the time and you get a lot of chicks." I said, "Well, shit, sign me up."

We actually considered two or three of the fraternities. One of them was a bunch of jocks, which, as I said, wasn't our scene. Another one was a bunch of Dilberts. That wasn't our scene either. But that first fraternity was like Goldilocks and the Three Bears. Just right. So I pledged to this fraternity, and felt really accepted for a change. They all liked me, and there wasn't one person in that fraternity who was "typecast." It really was like the movie *Animal House* because you had the Belushi guys, the James Widdoes guys, all kinds. Some fraternities would make you light a match, put it in your teeth, and say the Greek alphabet however many times the fraternity brother told you to say it before the match burned your lips. Our guys, they would always take things a step further than anybody else. These were the baddest sons-of-bitches on campus. I don't mean they were the meanest, I mean they were the coolest fucking fraternity. It was kind of an honor to be around those guys. Our fraternity brother would step up to the pledge, strike the match, put it between *his own* teeth, and tell you how many times to say the alphabet. If he burned his lip, he would beat the dog shit out of you. My big brother in the fraternity was a cool dude that I worshipped, who put me through the mill. He would take me by the ankles, turn me upside down, and hit my head on the porch. But I loved him and wanted to be just like him. Because of him, I got to where I could say the Greek alphabet three times before he burned his lip. I can still recite the Greek alphabet to this day.

Every year the fraternity held a dance called the Swamp Stomp. They'd gather up cane poles and put up this big fence around the backyard of the fraternity house. They'd hire a band—I actually played a time or two—wet the yard down to get it all muddy, and do a dance called the Gator where you'd get down in the mud, drunk, and flop around like you're an alligator up on the bank. They'd raise their mugs and sing drunk songs like fraternity guys would do. "Last night I stayed at home and masturbated. It felt so nice, I did it twice. It felt so neat, I used my feet." Shit like that. The song leader was a guy who had a big walrus mustache. He was kind of like Chuck Negron from Three Dog Night.

Anyway, there was this girl that went to school there. She was way too good for me, but I wanted her more than anything in the world. I didn't think she would ever talk to a dirtbag like me, but a friend of mine knew her and got her to say yes when I asked her to the Wine Festival, which happened every winter. This was literally like if I had asked Raquel Welch out at the time and she said yes. It was a big deal.

I didn't have a car, so we rode out there to the woods with a fraternity brother buddy and his girlfriend. He was a cat older than me who looked like James Dean and had a 1964 Plymouth Valiant that had a push-button transmission.

We didn't say a lot to each other on the way out there. It was like a blind date, even though I had met her a time or two. I was real nerved up. Here I was with my dream girl, who was wearing one of those sweaters that made her breasts look real good, and the only thing going through my mind was that I was going to sleep with her that night and that I was going to get good and shit-faced because I was nervous being around her. I told myself it was going to be okay if I was drunk.

For the Wine Festival they would take a bunch of number-ten washtubs out there in the middle of the woods where there were a few remaining metal pieces from an old abandoned fire tower with the concrete foundation still intact. Then they would get a bunch of blocks of ice from the icehouse, put them in the tubs, and pour them full of pure grain alcohol and punch. Everybody was supposed to bring their own glass or mug. Of course people would be drunk in about ten minutes, but that helped you out there in the Arkansas woods in winter because it was freezing cold. It was a stupid time to have a party in the woods, but that's what we did.

I had my Tupperware glass and started dipping it in the "wine," and the shit tasted like nothing. Within minutes I was so drunk I didn't even know who I was. The last thing I remember, I was lying in the backseat of my buddy's car in this chick's lap, and it was real cold. I saw the dome light on the ceiling of his car come on when he got in, but I was so drunk I felt like I was hallucinating. Everything was just spinning so fast.

When I came to, I was bleeding and lying facedown in the grass. Something real wet and sticky was all over me, and I had a big lump in my chest. I figured I'd either been shot or I had a huge tumor and it was bleeding. There was wet shit everywhere. I couldn't raise my head up, because I had a blazing headache, and my head was so heavy I couldn't get it up off the grass. I heard a football game going, so I thought, *I'm lying facedown in the grass at a football game*. I heard people yelling and cheering behind me, screaming at the ball game, and so I'm thinking I must be on the sidelines. Really I don't know what the fuck is going on. I finally managed to raise my head, and when I looked up there was a TV set about five or six feet in front of me and a ball game was on. I was lying facedown on the shag carpet in the fraternity house.

I turned around, and the whole fraternity was watching the

football game, and here I was, passed out in the middle of the fucking thing with matted-up, dried-up puke in my hair. When I tried to get up, everyone started yelling, "Get the fuck out of the way of the game!"

I looked down and saw I had a cheeseburger in my shirt that had separated. Buns on one side, mustard and ketchup on the other side, mayonnaise all over me. Later my buddies reconstructed the night for me. They said I had gotten so drunk I was trying to climb some tree out in the woods and then started trying to hump this girl. I had my britches down, running all around, and when they finally got me in the car to take me back to town, I puked all over her and all over the car. My buddy said I kept screaming at him that I was going to kill him if he didn't get me a cheeseburger. They said that I tried to climb over the seat to come after him. So he went and got me a cheeseburger, told me to go fuck myself, and threw it down my shirt. The girl just wanted to get the fuck away from me as soon as she could, so they took her back to her house, then took me back to the fraternity house and threw me on the floor with this cheeseburger in my shirt. I woke up the next day.

Years later I was trying to find a buddy of mine who was a fraternity brother there and probably my best friend in the whole outfit, so I just called. I'd been out of college for twenty-five years, but when I called and this guy answered the phone for the fraternity house there, I told him my name and he went, "Oh! Dude! The Cheeseburger Man!"

I dropped out of college and never did end up being a full fraternity member, but I had a great time with those guys.

CHAPTER THIRTEEN

"The Acid Room"

Why is everything so round?

Why do I hear that sound?

Who is that rainbow child?

Why's my imagination goin' wild?

I hear the music say

Why don't we fly away

I've never been this tall

Is that my face meltin' down the wall?

—"The Acid Room" (Thornton)

I TOOK TOO MUCH SHIT ONE TIME, AND THAT'S WHEN I KNEW THAT drugs were not my thing. When you get too high, you start thinking up crazy things that will help you come down. That night, not only did we do a lot of mushrooms, we were drunk, had been smoking pot, and took half a bottle of caffeine pills *before* we did the mushrooms.

I remember when I was first in California and somebody had a baggy of mushrooms. They said, "Hey, we're going to do some 'shrooms," which we didn't say because we were never big on cute words in Arkansas. We just said "mushrooms." At first I thought they were dried apricots. "*Those* are mushrooms?" I said. The guy said they were. I started to feel the baggy, and sure enough, they were all dried up.

We used to get mushrooms out of cow shit, and they were big old fluffy things. You would just take a bite out of a mushroom and then swallow something carbonated and the mushroom would just disintegrate in your mouth, kind of like malted milk balls. You're not really supposed to do that because there's strychnine in the stems, but we did anyway.

When I was in college, we knew a guy—someone I grew up with—who lived in the basement of some guy's house in Arkadelphia. He *seemed* real straitlaced—he looked like a golfer. But we also knew that he used to go out in the field to collect mushrooms and that he kept them in grocery bags in the refrigerator. One night we decided to pay him a visit.

By this time, I was living back at home in Malvern with my mom. I had a childhood buddy who was kind of like Stephen Wright, the comic—he had that kind of dry vibe about him. He picked me up in his Pontiac at my mom's house. We dropped by and picked up another buddy of mine who was a total pothead. Our destination was an Airstream trailer, owned by a buddy of mine who I used to roadie with sometimes. It was one of the smaller Airstreams, where you had to kind of walk sideways through the door to get into the bathroom. On our way to the trailer we went by the mushroom guy's place.

We had been drinking tall malt beverages all day long and smoking pot, which I don't do well with. I could do other shit and be fine, but if I smoked a joint, my heart would beat too fast and I would start thinking the FBI was after me. I *never* did well with it. Anyway, we had been smoking dope and drinking tall beers all day. I wanted to stay up all night, too, so I took some caffeine tablets. We went by that guy's place, and he gave us a paper grocery sack full of big, wet, fluffy mushrooms—sand, bugs, cow shit, the whole thing—and then we continued on to my buddy's little trailer house.

We sat in the living room, which was real small and had a little black-and-white TV with a coat-hanger antenna. In that same room there was this little stove where we cooked up some mushroom tea.

I drank a glass, but that wasn't enough. I really wanted to get fucked up. So I ate a few mushrooms and washed them down with a beer. See, I later learned that when people do mushrooms, they usually bite off a piece of this little apricot-looking thing. Well, that's not the kind of shit we did. We went way too far with it. I had already drunk a jelly jar full of this tea, which is some horrible stuff that tastes like horse shit, and I ate a couple of big mushrooms. This was *after* I had taken the caffeine tablets and was drunk and high all day.

The configuration in the room worked out so I was on this little tiny sofa thing and there was a guy sitting right next to me, then the other two guys were on chairs sitting close by. All this was in an area of about eight square feet or less.

When you're doing shit like this, there's a moment of panic that hits you, where you *know* you just fucked up and that you should not have done what you've just done. We were watching *The Honeymooners* or something on this coat-hanger television, and my friends started doing shit that I knew goddamn well they weren't really doing. One buddy was sitting right next to me, and I didn't want to look at him because I knew it was not going to look like him in a *bad* way. But I couldn't help it, and when I finally looked over, he was melting all over his chest. His face was just all the way down his chest. I could tell that none of them wanted to look at me either, so I closed my eyes. Suddenly, I was in a cartoon with Yosemite Sam. I was actually *in* the cartoon and I was running from Yosemite Sam. He was saying, "I'll blast you!" and all that kind of stuff. It's like, okay, closing my eyes is not going to help. Now, I had had some hallucinogenic experiences before—some bad, some good—and I knew that this one was not going to be good. When I talk to people who say, "Yeah, we did some acid and we did some mushrooms and then we went to the movies and laughed our asses off," I can't believe it. I'm like, "Wait a minute, you did acid *and* you drove to the movies?" We didn't have those experiences. We sat in a fucking closet talking to an eleven-foot caterpillar with a top hat on. If you're telling me that you went to the movies and laughed your asses off, you must have had different kind of shit than we had. We couldn't get out of the fucking room. We didn't dare. We went into a whole world where going outside and getting into a car never occurred to us because we didn't know it even existed. All that existed was right here in this fucking nightmare. We didn't laugh, it was *not* funny. And yet we kept doing it.

That night I started going into this dark place where I knew things were going to be bad, and that was only the beginning. As fast as I was speeding, and with all the shit that was happening when I closed my eyes and how my friends looked and what Ralph Kramden was doing, I knew fucking well that this was not going to end up good. It was going to be a long night, and this was just the kickoff. I figured if I could only get into the backseat of the car I'd be okay. So I walked out of this trailer, but I felt like I was that "keep on truckin'" cat with the leg that's a fucking mile and a half long. As I stepped out of the trailer it felt like my foot went down thirty feet. When I stepped onto the ground, it felt like this big fucking cotton ball. So I was walking in this cotton, and I saw the car. *If I can just get into the back-seat, everything will be okay.*

But the hood of the car looked only about a foot long while the rest of the car went all the way down to the end of the block. I was trying to get into the backseat, so I started scaling the car like Batman and Robin used to do when they were climbing a building. Finally, after what seems like hours, I got to the back door handle. I opened the door, which felt like it was made out of rubber, and the door started shaking like one of those tin things they used to use to make thunder in movies back in the old days. I got into the backseat, lay down, and sunk like twenty or thirty feet. Then I just puked *everywhere.*

I got up out of there and headed back to the trailer, the whole time with cartoons going off in my head. I opened the trailer door, which seemed fucking *huge* now, and my three buddies were in there running. Mind you, this whole trailer is probably like twenty feet, and they're literally in single file running from the living room to this little bedroom, throwing themselves onto the bed on top of one another, then getting up and running back to the living room. They were doing this over and over. I got in line with them and started running back and forth behind them. We did this for God knows how long until we finally went back and sat in the living room. One of my buddies started crying and telling this awful story. *All* my buddies started looking kind of like pigs. Their noses were turned up, and they had these big, hollow eyes.

I went into the bathroom, which had a lightbulb in front of the mirror with a chain on it. At that time I was even skinnier than I am now, with long hair and sunken eyes. I turned on the light, and I looked at myself in the mirror. Big fucking mistake. The mirror was about an inch from my face, and I looked exactly like that guy from *Beauty and the Beast*. Not the cartoon, the French version. I don't mean *kind of* looked like that, I mean I *was* that guy. Well, that freaked me out.

Finally I told my buddy that we had to get back to town. We got in his car and tried to drive the twenty-seven miles back into town. Whenever we went around a curve, the road became a rubber band—the road would go way the fuck out there like in a cartoon. I said to my buddy, "Are you really able to do this?" And he said, "For some reason, I am." And so we got back to town.

It was already dawn, about six thirty in the morning. Everything looked real yellow to me. I had just finished with this rubber-band ride, my buddy still looked like a pig with hollowed-out eyes, and the whole world was yellow. I lived over at my mom's house at the time, and I didn't want to go home real fucked up. I didn't want to go to my buddy's house either, because his parents were real fucking *not* fun and they didn't like me anyway, high or not. In this fog, I told my buddy to take me to this guy's house—this guy I used to be in a band with when I was in junior high but probably hadn't seen in three or four years. The last time I saw him I chewed his ass out, then got him down on the ground in a choke hold, threatening him because he stole a bunch of my brother's records. For some reason I told my buddy, "Take me over there, I want to hang out with him today."

He dropped me off, and I went up the stairs to this cat's place. Somehow I knew he had a stand-up job now and was living in this duplex apartment, married, like a regular Joe—and when I knocked on the door his wife answered. I knew her a little bit, she was a couple of years behind me in school. She opened the door and looked at me like, *What in the fuck are you doing standing in my doorway?* But she just said, "Hi." God knows how I looked. I had long stringy hair that was probably greasy, and I was wearing some kind of shit that said Allman Brothers—I had painted it on there myself—and I go, "Hey, how you doing?" And she goes, "Fine." And I said, "Hey, is *the guy* here?" She goes, "Yeah."

He came up behind her, and he didn't have a shirt on. They had just gotten up and were making breakfast. I could smell bacon and hear it crackling. He goes, "Hey, so . . . what's up?"

"Oh, I just came by to see you." Well, who the fuck "comes by to see you" at seven in the morning looking like I did? But he just said, "You want to come in?"

"Yeah."

"We're having breakfast, you want anything?"

"No, that's okay."

And they were just staring at me like, as my buddy Jim Varney used to say, a pig staring at a wristwatch—like, *Why is this guy at my fucking apartment?* But the guy invited me in and said, "Well, have a seat."

They sat down and had breakfast for like thirty or forty minutes while I sat there about twelve feet away from them. They were real quiet. The news was on, and we were all just kind of watching it, but I knew they were thinking, *What is he* doing *here? Has he turned into a fucking lunatic? Is he going to stab us?*

They finished breakfast and went and got ready for work—she worked at a department store, and he worked at a real estate office or something. They came out into the living room, and I was still just sitting there. One of them, I can't remember which, said, "Listen, we're going to work now. Did you want to stay here, or were you going to go?" I said, "If you don't mind, I'll just wait until you guys get off work." They said okay, but I could see they were nervous. They were nice people, other than the time he ripped the albums off and I choked him.

So they went off to work and I got into their bed, which was unmade and smelled like "other people." I lay facedown and passed out into this sort of psychedelic world that was kind of the leftover effect from the night before. When I came to, I heard people in the kitchen and plates clanking. I had been asleep all day, and they had come home and were making supper. I got up and walked into the kitchen, drool going down my chin, and they were sitting down to eat again. I said, "Hey, guys, thanks for letting me hang."

"Well, yeah, it was good to see you."

"Yeah, it was good to see you guys too."

The guy got up and walked me to the door. He said, "Okay, well, see you around."

"Yeah, see you around."

I walked down the stairs feeling kind of weird. Everybody still looked a little bit funny. I was several miles away from my house, so I just started walking. On the way, I went by this trailer where this girl, who had the most perfect legs I'd ever seen in my life, lived with her mom. I always wanted to get with that girl, and for some reason I thought this might be the time. So I stopped by there and knocked on the door. The girl I barely knew but always wanted to hook up with answered and let me in.

I hung out with her for a few hours, but I was too much in another world to even ask her about anything meaningful. I talked to her for a while, and she just looked at me. Then I finally walked home, and I ended up sitting outside my house for three days. I mean, I would go in at night, sleep, talk to my mom a little bit, but mainly I just sat outside on this concrete square where there was a basketball hoop, thinking that my life was over. Everything still looked really yellow and I was real depressed. My Boston terrier, Butch, sat next to me. You could see tears in his eyes. He was real sensitive and would actually cry when you were upset. He knew something was wrong with me.

I sat there in this depression for three days, after which I decided that I was never going to be a drug addict. That life was not for me. It wasn't the actual day I quit, but it was the day I decided that I was not going to be a drug addict.

"THE TOM EPPERSON STORY" BY TOM EPPERSON
(AS TOLD TO TOM EPPERSON)

Part III

I didn't see Billy for years after I went away to college. When I finished my master's, I came back to Malvern, where I worked on a novel and tried to figure out what to do next, and Billy and I reestablished contact. He no longer looked like Ernie Douglas. He had a beard, tattoos, and hair down to his shoulders. He sang and played drums in a rock band, while working a series of crummy factory and construction jobs. Like me, Billy had large ambitions. I wanted to be the next Vladimir Nabokov. He wanted to be the next Elvis Presley.

CHAPTER FOURTEEN

Dear Billy Bob

"Maybe tomorrow" is the mantra for me
Even though I know it's just a fantasy.
But somethin' 'bout hopin' keeps us healthier
Bankin' on your dreams can make you wealthier I hear.

—"Somewhere Down the Road"

(Thornton/Andrew)

THERE WAS A COUNTRY DUO IN THE FIFTIES AND SIXTIES FROM HOT Springs, Arkansas, called the Wilburn Brothers. I always loved them. Their act used to be the whole Wilburn family, but later it became just Teddy and Doyle. They looked just alike—all the Wilburns looked alike—and they wore these sparkly suits. They had a bunch of big hits, and they even had their own TV show on Saturday afternoons. They gave Loretta Lynn her start, and just like Dolly Parton came to be known as "that girl on *The Porter Wagoner Show*," Loretta Lynn came to be known on *The Wilburn Brothers Show*. There are a few actors from Arkansas like me, Alan Ladd, and Dick Powell, but if you boiled it down, of all the famous people from Arkansas, most of them came from country music. Guys like Jim Ed Brown and the Wilburns.

Everywhere Tom and I ever went, from New York to Mexico, San Diego, L.A., all those places, we never went anywhere we knew anybody or had any money. We didn't do anything right, ever. We made plans to go to Nashville, get a cheap-ass hotel room, and just start walking up and down Music Row, going into places and announcing, "Hey! We're songwriters!" It's like, "Really? You came to Nashville to be songwriters? What an interesting idea, we never heard of *that* shit before."

We had a bunch of songs we planned to bring with us—songs like "Crop Dusting Man." We were trying to make one of those novelty songs kind of like Jim Stafford or someone would do. There was a song by Terry Fell called "Truck Driving Man," and we thought, *What if we just took some stupid-ass profession and did "Something Man"—"Plumbing Man" or whatever?* We decided on "Crop Dusting Man." *We* thought it was funny anyway.

When I told my mom that we were going to Nashville, she said, "You should look up the Wilburns." My mother knew the Wilburns from when they would come to Alpine as little kids. They would play at the Presbyterian church, which was right across the road from my grandmother's house, and they even sort of used my grandmother's house as a dressing room. My mom had a crush on Teddy Wilburn when he was, like, twelve and she was maybe ten. So there was a connection in Nashville—a loose one, but stronger than we had any other place we went.

We arrived in Nashville and went to have lunch at a place called the Merchant's Café, which I think is still there. We were in there and we saw a stocky guy, built like Raymond Burr. He had a lot of hair and glasses. We thought he was an old man at the time, but he was probably fifteen years younger than I am now. He looked like a novelist type, and you could tell he was writing a book. He had all his shit spread out all over the table. He would write a little bit, run his fingers through his hair, then write some more. I'll never forget the image of his baseball mitt–looking hands, fingers running through his greasy hair, flopping it back, shaking his head. This guy was sitting there looking angry, like he wanted to shoot himself, and it's like, goddamn. We had just gotten there to be writers, and here's the first guy we see in the Merchant's Café and he looks like he's going to hang himself tonight.

We finished up our lunch and went to look for the Wilburns' publishing company, Surefire Music. We found it over on Music Row West. We walked in, and their secretary was sitting there. I said, "Hey! We're here to be songwriters, and my mom used to know Teddy Wilburn. They used to change clothes at my grandmother's house."

She wasn't really paying attention, and I thought she was going to give us the bum's rush, but she said, "Teddy and Doyle, they're not here. You say you know them?" I said, "Yes, ma'am, yes, ma'am." She said, "Well, Doyle will be back here in a little while."

When we learned Doyle Wilburn wasn't going to be in until after lunch, Tom and I went walking down the street, and Tom said, "Let's get a hooker." Tom and I, we were never into hookers. Me, I always loved women, but I never looked at hookers and strippers as people I would hook up with. No judgment, it's just I was too nervous about it. I couldn't really even go into strip joints. I've been to a handful of strip joints in my lifetime, but I just don't know where to look—their eyes, their breasts, below their waists, I just don't know. They're sad places for me. I never got into them. But there was a time when Tom and I wanted to try out what it was like *to get* a hooker.

First try at it, I think, might have been in Nashville. It could have been in Dallas, but both attempts took place pretty close together. We walked over to a place that somebody may have told us about, I don't remember, but it was a brick building in a decent neighborhood by Music Row. It looked like a dentist's office, and it had a plaque in brass or something on the door that said ATHLETIC CLUB.

We looked at each other like, *Huh*. That's *supposed to be the deal*. So we knocked on the door, and a woman, who was obviously a hooker, opened the door. We stood looking at her for a few seconds, and Tom whispered, "Ask her . . . *say* something," because my buddy Tom, he never talks. He doesn't talk to anybody. So *I* had to do the talking. "Uh, yeah, we'd like to lift some weights," I said.

She looked at us like, *The fuck? What planet did you motherfuckers come from?* but just goes, "What?" I said, "Yeah, we just wanted to come in and work out on some weights." And she said, "Who *are* you? Get the fuck out of here!" and just slammed the door on us.

We walked around for a little bit, then went back to Surefire Music. I think Doyle came out in the midst of this. I said something to Doyle, and I wrote a note to Teddy. Nothing really happened then.

Sometime in 1979, I went back to Nashville, this time by myself. And *this* time I thought ahead. I had written to them and even talked to Teddy on the phone. I told him the whole story about my grandmother and my mom, and he invited me to come.

By then, I was playing in Nothin' Doin', which I mentioned earlier. I had written a few songs that I took with me to Teddy's studio, where he was working on a record of Don Williams songs. He was a real slick cat, all put together with his hair gassed back and wearing fancy clothes. He was a cool guy. At that point, I'd never been in a studio that had huge walls with big speakers where you could turn the sound up to supersonic levels. He was playing this new record of Don Williams's songs.

Then we had a nice talk. I told him all about my band and about how I wanted to be a songwriter, and he goes, "Hey, let's go take a ride in the limo." I'm like, wow, we're going to take a ride in the limo. It was an old limousine, probably from the sixties, and I thought he'd have some guy named Jeeves that was going to take us around town, but Teddy got in the driver's seat and I walked around to the passenger's seat. He drove me all over Nashville, telling me everything that happened in that town. He told me where Hank Williams did this over here and Ray Price did that over there, and where Hank and Audrey lived.

Anyway, while we were out there cruising, he said, "I got the funniest feeling about you. I meet young guys, they come up here all the time, and I don't know what it's gonna be, but you're going to be a well-known guy. I think there's something different about you. You're going to do really well one day."

A couple of months later, Teddy wrote me a letter on the Wilburn Brothers gold letterhead. He began the letter, "Dear Billy Bob," and in parentheses, "(which I think you should use instead of just Billy)." He talked to me a little bit about that when I was with him. He said, "You know, people will always remember that name. Nobody will ever have to ask who you are." I was just Billy to that point in my life. I was never called Billy Bob, because back in Arkansas you don't call yourself that. You might as well just say Jethro Bodine. Because of Teddy Wilburn, I used my full name, and sure enough, even when I first got to L.A., there wasn't a fucking soul among the casting directors who didn't know who I was when I called.

Anyway, he wrote me this letter that said, "If Surefire Music can help you out, that'd be great. We really like your songs, [blah blah blah]. Teddy Wilburn, God's Love, '79." I'm Billy Bob because of Teddy Wilburn. And I still have that letter.

CHAPTER FIFTEEN

"Breakin' Down"

Let go of the wheel, the drivin's done

Don't turn around

You showed up in the lost and found

Welcome to our town

Just close your eyes, you're finally breakin' down

—"Breakin' Down" (Thornton/Andrew)

BEFORE I CAME TO CALIFORNIA, TOM EPPERSON AND I WENT TO NEW York to seek our fame and fortune. It was 1977, and we stayed ten hours. We had a tape recorder with us because we wanted to record our reaction to seeing New York City. Tom says that he still has the cassette tape and that we sound so fucking country you can't believe it.

I spent ten, fifteen years in California reading for parts they wouldn't give me unless it was about a redneck. But there have been a million New Yorkers playing in movies about Mississippi, and they have that Foghorn Leghorn accent that doesn't exist anywhere. I grew up in the South, and I never heard anybody talk like that. There are some people in Georgia and Alabama that give it a little lilt, but not *that* much. Anyway, it's not like I sound like Charles Boyer now, but at least if I have to do a movie where I'm *not* from the South, I can do it. Back then, we were just hillbillies. I haven't heard the tape since 1977, but Tom says *you can't imagine* how country we sound. He says he and I were hyperventilating as we arrived in New York before we went into a tunnel. We were coming into town from Pennsylvania, or New Jersey probably. We came out of this tunnel, and I remember we parked not too far out on Sixth Avenue. When we saw the Statue of Liberty, we started yelling, "Jesus Christ, look at that, that's the Statue of Liberty, and it's green! It's fucking green!" Tom says you can hear me breathing too hard, hyperventilating on tape. I haven't heard this tape in thirty fucking years, you know, but on that tape is exactly what the fuck I said the first time I ever left home. I would be embarrassed to hear it now.

"THE TOM EPPERSON STORY" BY TOM EPPERSON
(AS TOLD TO TOM EPPERSON)

Part IV

I was a big fan of *The Waltons* and identified with John Boy, the aspiring young Southern writer. When John Boy left Walton's Mountain and moved to New York City to seek his fame and fortune, I decided it was a sign that I should do the same. I talked Billy into coming with me. The fact that we had very little money and not a single contact in New York didn't seem to faze us. We warned our weeping mothers and girlfriends that it would probably be years before we returned, then bought a road map and left Malvern in my packed-to-the-gills black Buick.

It was June 1977. The Summer of Sam. We drove through the very intimidating Holland Tunnel and parked the car on the Avenue of the Americas. We began to walk. New York terrified us. The buildings seemed miles high. Wave on wave of yellow taxis rushed hither and thither down the streets. The throngs of pedestrians seemed alien, rude, and in a great hurry. The only friendly person we encountered was a chubby black woman who said to me: "Hey, baby, wanna date?" Flattered, I replied: "No, ma'am, but thanks for asking."

We walked and walked, and day turned into night, and a violent thunderstorm struck the city, and we were soaked to the skin, and we saw apocalyptic-looking clouds whipping past the top of the Empire State Building. We decided to return to the car, but weren't sure where we had left it. We became lost. The rain continued. We were afraid the Son of Sam was going to get us. Finally, with the help of a kindly cabdriver, we found our car. We'd arrived in New York at noon. We left at ten o'clock that night. Shaken and humiliated, we took our time driving back to Arkansas. We hung out in a cheap motel in Rehoboth Beach, Delaware, for a few days. Twelve days after we'd left, we were back in Malvern. Billy went to the Dairy Queen. He ran into his girlfriend. She was surprised. She said: "But I thought you were goin' to New York City."

Youth is nothing, though, if not resilient, and after a few weeks of recuperation, we hit the road again. We boarded a Greyhound bus to Lakeside, a suburb of San Diego, to visit Billy's aunt and uncle, Sally and Bill.

CHAPTER SIXTEEN

"Pie in the Sky"

I'm pretty sure I'm gonna come up with a plan fairly soon

Lately at night I've been talkin' it over with the man in the moon

I've got this crazy feelin' that my ship will come in

Maybe fate will finally flip this old loser a win

I keep throwin' wishes

In a well that's almost dry

I'm keepin' body and soul together

Eatin' pie in the sky

—"Pie in the Sky" (Thornton/Andrew)

WE CAME BACK TO ARKANSAS WITH OUR TAILS BETWEEN OUR LEGS, and then Tom wanted to go to Hollywood to be a screenwriter. Instead, we headed to San Diego to stay with my aunt Sally and my uncle Bill because we were afraid of Hollywood. The truth is, we were *always* too afraid to go to L.A., so we'd go to other places first. We kinda *crept* into L.A.

I've always maintained that you really haven't lived until you've taken a cross-country trip on a bus, and that's how we traveled to San Diego. On the way, we stopped at a bus stop in Sweetwater, Texas, and I ate this peach cobbler that *looked* great but—you know how real cobbler, good cobbler, has a crust on it and there's crunchy shit? Well, *this* was just balls of white dough with peaches in it, in some kind of soupy sauce. I don't know if that's what did it or not.

We got back on the bus, and from Sweetwater to El Paso there ain't a fucking thing. It was night, dark as shit, and when you looked out the window of the bus, you literally couldn't see anything. Tom and I were sitting about three-quarters of the way back, and there was this girl up front who was kind of hot. I kept telling Tom, "I'm gonna go over there and sit next to that girl." So Tom said, "Why don't you just go sit by her?" and I said, "I don't know . . ." Truth is, I was feeling a little queasy.

I finally went down and sat by her, and we started talking. "Hey, where you from?" and all that sort of shit. All of a sudden, my stomach started making the weirdest noises—it was real loud—and I got the shits like you can't imagine. The kind that feels like knives are being stuck in your intestines. I broke out in a cold sweat, and I go, "Uh, yeah, I'll be right back, I'll talk to you in a little bit." I got up and walked down the aisle with my ass pinched together because I was about to shit myself right in the seat. I walked all the way back down the bus toward the bathroom, which was in the back corner. Right outside the door there were two seats that were kind of smaller than the rest of the seats. Just on the outside of the bathroom, there was an old black couple, and the man looked like Tom Epperson's dad—he was exactly Tom's dad, only he was black.

Anyway, when I got there, the bathroom door just kind of came open. I went in and closed the door, which had no lock on it—the latch and lock were both broken. It just had a little bitty knob that you had to hold with two fingers to keep the fucking thing shut. I pull my pants down and I'm shitting all the way down to the toilet.

So, I'm down there, miserable, cramps, pains like you can't imagine. I'm in there forever moaning, *"Ohhhhh! Oh man!"* just shitting like crazy. I'm sweating and cold, and people keep coming to the door trying to open it. I got this one little knob to hold on to and I'm screaming, *"I'm in here!"* It would open like a foot and I would have to pull it back.

Finally, when I was done—though the pain kind of never went away—I got up, and there's no toilet paper or paper towels left. There's not a fucking thing in the bathroom but shit on the walls and the floor. I panicked. *What am I gonna do?* I pulled my pants and underwear off and wiped my ass and legs as well as I could with my underwear—which was not very thoroughly— and threw my underwear in the trash. *That's* where all the paper towels were.

I pulled my pants back up, and I went out there devastated, just fucking devastated. I was as skinny then as I am now, maybe skinnier, and right at that moment I felt like I weighed about eighty fucking pounds. So I went back out there and sat down by Tom, and I'm like, "Aw gee, I was real sick . . ." A truck driver was sitting behind us, and he offered us whiskey, so we drank whiskey with him.

The next stop was Big Spring, Texas. We got off, and the girl was still wanting to talk to me. It was two o'clock in the morning, and we went into this dingy café that was gray and yellow. The girl was like, "Hey, you want to get some pie?" And I said, "I don't know . . ." and I went right into the bathroom to clean myself up some more.

Before you knew it, we were getting back on the bus, and we arrived in San Diego at sunrise. When we got there, my ass was on fire. I was like one of those baboons with the raw-looking asses, and I still smelled like shit, but when I got to my aunt's house, I had the best shower I ever had in my life.

WE SPENT THREE MONTHS LIVING IN MY AUNT AND UNCLE'S TOOLSHED kind of thing that had a water bed, sharing the place with this old Mexican man who was doing the tile on their pool. He had these nightmares, and Tom and I were afraid that he was like Juan Corona and that we'd wake up with a machete in our faces in the middle of the fucking night. You'd wake up and freeze your fucking ass off floating on that goddamn water bed. I woke up with a sore throat and a cold every morning listening to nightmares in Spanish.

We stayed in San Diego for three or four months and Tom ended up getting engaged to a Mexican girl in Tecate, Mexico. I got her sister's name tattooed on me.

"THE TOM EPPERSON STORY" BY TOM EPPERSON
(AS TOLD TO TOM EPPERSON)

Part V

We fell in love with California as soon as we stepped off the bus. The mountains, the palm trees, the ocean, all seemed magic to us. Billy's uncle Bill worked as a border guard at Tecate, the Mexican town east of Tijuana where the beer comes from. One Sunday afternoon, Billy and I went to Tecate with Billy and Sally and their teenage children, and we found ourselves in the midst of a fiesta. We saw two beautiful Mexican girls looking at us and smiling. We introduced ourselves. They turned out to be sisters. Rosa, who was seventeen, knew a little English. Guillermina, nineteen, knew none at all. We instantly fell in love, Billy with Rosa and me with Guillermina, and decided to move to Lakeside. We took the bus across the country back to Malvern, packed up the Buick again, then set out for a new life in California.

The Eagles were our favorite group, and "Hotel California" was constantly playing on the radio, which we took as a sign that this was all meant to be. We got an apartment on Wintergarden Boulevard.

Strangely, both our heroes, Presley and Nabokov, died within the first month of our living there. We took that as a sign too, though we weren't sure of what.

We drove over a winding mountain road to Tecate every chance we got. We met Rosa and Guillermina's very large family. There were nine daughters, all beautiful, but Rosa and Guillermina were the most beautiful. The family was very poor. They got their water in buckets from a well. The toilet was an outhouse. But they couldn't have been any more welcoming and warm to us, and I spent in that house some of the best hours of my life. I asked Guillermina to marry me, and she said yes.

But back in Lakeside things were not so fun. What little money we'd brought from Arkansas was running out fast. We didn't have any luck finding jobs. And as often happened with Billy and me when we were under pressure, we began to fight with each other. After a couple of months Billy had had enough and took a bus back to Arkansas. And that was the end of the line for him and Rosa.

I managed to stick it out a little longer. I got a job as a night clerk in a convenience store for two bucks an hour. Billy and I had somehow escaped the clutches of the Son of Sam in New York, but somebody was going around robbing and shooting convenience store clerks in the Lakeside area, so every night in UtoteM was a long and scary journey to dawn. The mountains and Mexico and Guillermina were great, but my situation became untenable when I got laid off by UtoteM around Christmas. I couldn't even cut it as a convenience store clerk. So I hatched a new plan. I would return to Arkansas, go back to college for a semester and get certified to teach in high school, get a job and make some money, then go back to Mexico and marry Guillermina, then bring her back to Arkansas. All of which I almost did.

A year later found me in Augusta, a tiny town in the middle of the cotton fields of east Arkansas. I thought it a bleak and lonely place. Before it turned cold, the mosquitoes would be so thick around the streetlights at night that they looked like smoke. And then winter came, and the fields were dull and dreary and dead and endless.

I was the ninth-grade English teacher at Augusta High School. In three weeks, Guillermina and I were going to be married, in Tecate, in a Catholic church, and then I would be bringing her back to Augusta. And then I was summoned, via an ominous intercom message, to the principal's office.

As in some noir movie or novel, I walked through the door of the office and found trouble in the personage of a very pretty girl sitting demurely across the desk from my principal, Mr. Matlock. Mr. Matlock explained to me that the pretty girl was a senior in college and was being assigned to my class as a practice teacher.

I became immediately smitten with the girl, and my smittenness was reciprocated. Guillermina and her family didn't have a phone, so I wrote her a letter (partially in Spanish— each of us had been studying the other's language) telling her that I'd realized I was too young and immature to be married (which was quite true) and that I wouldn't be coming to Tecate for the wedding. In a few days, I received a collect phone call from Guillermina. Rosa was on the line too, to act as our translator. Guillermina wasn't sure she understood what the letter meant. I started with the too young and immature thing again, but Guillermina wasn't buying it. Finally I admitted that I'd met somebody else. By this time I was crying, and Rosa, as she translated for us, was also crying, but Guillermina didn't cry. She said a simple but devastating sentence to me in her newly acquired English: "I have a dress white." Guillermina and Rosa were so beautiful and so sweet and deserved so much more than they got from Billy and me. I often wonder what became of them.

From a cosmic justice standpoint, things worked out. Two months after our romance began, my practice teacher, who had returned to classes at her college, disappeared. After several frantic days, I tracked her down. She informed me that she felt we had entered into a relationship too hastily and that it was over between us. Then I got another one of those ominous calls to the principal's office and was told by Mr. Matlock (six-foot-nine, the former basketball coach) that the school board had decided not to renew my contract (I never really fit in in Augusta), and then a few weeks later I found out they'd hired my practice teacher to replace me!

I moved to Little Rock. Rented the bottom half of a dumpy duplex in a bad neighborhood near downtown, just up the hill from a liquor store. (The down-and-up walk between duplex and liquor store would be made with increasing frequency over the next two years.) I began piecing together a living. I wrote some articles for a couple of local magazines, taught freshman English part-time at a couple of colleges, and had a six-month stint as the editor of a weekly newspaper called *The Voice,* where I made history. (When I quit to take another job, the publisher told me: "You've been the worst editor in the paper's history.")

Meanwhile, I was writing. From when I'd begun during my freshman year, I'd written two novels, dozens of short stories, and hundreds of poems. But with the exception of five or six poems and a single short story, none of it had been published. I'd diligently been sending my stuff out but had been met with a blizzard of rejection slips. I was nearing thirty and was barely making enough money to keep a roof over my head. And here I was stuck back in Arkansas when I had wanted to venture forth and explore the world. So I conceived a new plan.

I would move to Los Angeles and become a Hollywood writer. Going back to *Attack of the Crab Monsters,* I'd always loved movies and was confident I could write them.

But it felt too daunting to tackle this task by myself. I wanted a partner.

Billy was living back in Malvern. When he'd returned from California, he'd settled down a bit. One of his mother's friends was the secretary of the dynamic first-term governor of Arkansas, hardly older than me, Bill Clinton. Strings were pulled, and Billy got hired on at the highway department.

We'd parted on such bad terms in Lakeside, I didn't think we'd ever speak to each other again. I would go back to Malvern pretty often to see my mother. (My father had died years before, a victim of obesity, cigarettes, and alcohol.) My mother and Billy's mother were best friends. I'd run into Billy sometimes. We began to hang out again. After a while we were back to being best buddies.

He was still playing in a band, a ZZ Tops–like group called Tres Hombres. But in terms of getting a career going, he'd been about as successful musically as I'd been litera-turely. Billy had a lot of charisma as a stage performer, and he'd done some acting in high school. His marriage broke up, which meant he was free to travel again, so I tried to convince him to come out to California with me and become an actor. (I don't remember this, but Billy has told me that as part of my persuasion campaign I kept telling him he looked just like John Travolta.)

Except for songs, Billy hadn't done any writing, but he had a great way with words. He was always having bizarre adventures and telling hilarious stories about them, where he'd provide the voices for all the different characters. He, too, was a movie lover, so we decided to write scripts to-gether. I went to the library and checked out a how-to book on screenwriting, along with the screenplay for *The Exor-*

cist. In the spring of 1981 we wrote a script called "Run for the Hills," about a star high school quarterback who gets in trouble with the law and has to go on the run. (It was a very bad script with patches of very good writing, and later proved useful as a writing sample.) Then we started making plans to return to the West Coast.

I was teaching freshman English at UALR, so we had to wait for the semester to end. We used to climb to the roof of Billy's house with a six-pack of beer, and we'd watch white clouds drift across the blue sky and drink and dream about all the wonderful things waiting for us in California. We were absolutely positive that we were going to be big successes, that we were going to tear Hollywood apart. We were pretty sure it would all happen by Christmas.

The semester ended. Billy quit his job at the highway department. After the usual tearful good-byes with our mothers, we left Malvern on a rainy Friday morning in early June. We had a tape player, and we put in a Beach Boys cassette so that "California Girls" was playing as we pulled out of town, with the windshield wipers sloshing back and forth.

I had traded in my black Buick for a sky-blue Mustang. We stopped off at a gas station and bought a road map. We had $500 between us. When we reached L.A. after three days of traveling, we had $400.

CHAPTER SEVENTEEN

"An Island of My Own"

There's no trees, no sand, no sky
In this loser's paradise
But it was cheap enough to buy
I guess you'd say I set the price
Lookin' at the wild rough sea
Where souls like mine are grown
I've washed up on an island of my own

—"An Island of My Own" (Thornton/Andrew)

NOW, YOU GOT TO UNDERSTAND THAT TOM AND I WERE NOT EVEN living in Hollywood yet. We ran out of money. When we first got to L.A., we had $500 and Tom's old beat-up Mustang. Remember when Mustangs were ugly? There were like three or four years in the late 1970s when Mustangs were ugly as shit.

Every night when we were looking for jobs, we stayed in a different motel. The first one we stayed at was in Inglewood near the airport, with airplanes taking off every night. Then we went to Westchester for three or four nights, then Santa Monica for a couple of nights. We stayed all over the place, until we had $20 left, not even enough to stay at a motel. Tom and I drove out to Santa Monica, and we were sitting on the Santa Monica pier with $20. We were officially street people that day in 1981.

We were there sitting on this bench where the telescopes are looking out over the ocean, and we had nothing. You know how sometimes when things are just over and you're literally at the bottom of the barrel and then there's a certain calm? People who have had a gun to their head and ended up living through it somehow have described that feeling, and they say, "Once the gun was to my head and it was cocked, I had this calm—it's like, this is it, this is my last day." Well, we had that.

We were sitting next to this old man, old even by our standards now. He was probably late eighties or something and looked like pictures you've seen of Karl Marx, with a long beard. He had a little hat on and was sketching with a pencil as he looked out at the ocean. He knew just enough English to communicate with us, and we got enough out of him to know that he was from Russia and lived out in the Wilshire District downtown with his sister. His visa was about to run out, and he was going to have to go back to Russia. He was very sad because he loved his sister and he loved this country. He didn't want to leave America. So he ended up sketching pictures of me and Tom. Tom still has the one he drew of him. Me, I lose every fucking thing.

So the three of us were sitting on this bench looking out on the ocean. Tom and I were going to have to go away, the Russian guy was going to have to go away, we had twenty bucks, he had nothing. We didn't have a way to get out of town and back to Arkansas. We had no idea what we were going to do.

I knew I had a $500 check coming from the Arkansas Highway Department from when I shoveled asphalt for them just before we came out to California. They owed me that much on my retirement fund, which you pay into when you start working for them. So that was going to come *sometime,* we just didn't know when.

"THE TOM EPPERSON STORY" BY TOM EPPERSON
(AS TOLD TO TOM EPPERSON)
Part VI

It was my intention to follow in my dad's footsteps and become a lawyer, but when I got to college, I changed my mind. I had a wonderful freshman English teacher named George Horneker, who thought I had talent as a writer. Late in my freshman year, I decided to change my major from political science to English. I felt it was my destiny to be a writer, and I've never looked back or had one second of self-doubt since then.

I got a BA from the University of Arkansas at Little Rock, and an MA from the University of Arkansas at Fayetteville, and then I applied to and was accepted by the PhD program at the University of Texas at Austin. My plan was to become a college professor. I'd taught freshman English as a grad student at Fayetteville and enjoyed teaching, and I loved the calm campuses and pretty coeds and hushed libraries of academia. It seemed like a good way to make a living until my writing started to pay off. But then I changed my mind again.

I'd lived my life almost exclusively in the world of books, and I realized that, both as a writer and a person, I needed to experience more of what some have called the "real" world. I wrote Texas and told them I wasn't coming.

Exploring the world can be a daunting task, especially when you're the shy, quiet type like I was. Fortunately, I found a partner.

But Los Angeles was gigantic. We didn't know a soul. Used to Arkansas prices, we'd thought we had plenty of money to get us into an apartment. That assumption proved incorrect. We'd arrived in the middle of a scorching heat wave. Indeed, that June turned out to be the hottest in L.A.'s history. We drove around in my un-air-conditioned car sweating through our clothes and searching for an apartment and for jobs that didn't seem to exist. We moved from cheap motel to cheaper motel and became increasingly desperate as we watched our money running out. Ten days after we'd got there, we were down to $20. Not enough for another night at the motel in Westchester near the airport we were staying at. We packed up our car and left.

We drove to the ocean. We went out on the Santa Monica Pier, sat down on a bench, and tried to figure out what to do. We didn't have the money to get back home. We could call up our mothers (collect) and have them send us some money, but that thought was horrible. It would be New York all over again. Leaving with much fanfare to seek our fortunes in the big city, then sneaking back into town only a couple of weeks after we'd left. We sat there for hours. The sun began to go down in Santa Monica Bay.

"You know, Tom," I said, "my cousin Jane lives out in Rialto. I haven't seen her since I was a kid, but maybe we could go there and stay."

So I make a collect call to my cousin Jane, who's married to this guy Nick, a truck driver. They had been married forever. They're my cousins, but they were, like, older cousins—more like an aunt and uncle to me. They had kids and everything, so I felt bad about calling people who I never call and imposing on them. But I didn't know what else to do, they were the closest people I knew.

I said, "Can we come out and see you?" but not *stay* with you, and they say, "Yeah, we would be happy to see you."

We went out there and slept in their garage. Tom slept on the pool table, and I slept *under* the pool table. Tom's four years older than me, so he always got the best seat in the house.

CHAPTER EIGHTEEN

Rewriting *Othello*: The Othie and Desi Show

THERE WAS ONE GUY WE KNEW TO CALL IN L.A., THIS GUY JEFF LES-ter, who was playing a deputy in a TV series based on the movie *Walking Tall*. Tom was a substitute teacher back in Arkansas and had taught with Jeff's girlfriend's mother. (The girlfriend had a part in the TV series too.)

Jeff was real nice to us. Tom and I told him we had written a screenplay that wasn't worth a shit—I mean, the writing was pretty good, but it was like 190 pages long and structured *totally* wrong. We didn't know what we were doing, but Jeff said, "Why don't you just come to this acting class and check it out?" And I said, "How much does it cost? I don't have any money." And he said, "You can just audit the class."

I didn't know shit about any of what was going on in that class. There was one chick in there that I had seen on a commercial, so, to me, she was like fucking Laurence Olivier. This acting class was taught by a guy named John Widlock, who I thank every day of my life. I can trace everything I'm doing now, any success I've ever had, to that acting class at Crossroads of the World, Maudie Treadway, and Billy Wilder, who I'll get to later, because of one simple thing: encouragement.

I didn't start out to be an actor. I was in a rock-and-roll band, and I played baseball. But to this day—and I've had different acting coaches and teachers over the years—I've never seen an acting teacher or an acting class make a bad actor good. I have, however, seen acting teachers make a good actor worse. A lot of acting teachers take you from point A to point Z by going through point Q, as opposed to going straight for point Z. What I mean by that is—and if you live in L.A., you understand—if I'm living here in Beverly Hills and I want to get to Glendale, I don't go through Downey to get to Glendale, I go straight to Glendale.

The point of acting, if you're looking to do *good* acting, is to be realistic, to make it look *natural*. If you're *studying* to be natural, you've already fucked up. It's like somebody's telling you to take a creative writing course. How do you teach someone to be a *creative* writer? It's not possible. It's like the old joke about military intelligence. So if an acting teacher says, "I'm going to teach you how to be natural," then you're screwed.

I speak at different acting groups sometimes, and acting teachers *love* it when the first thing I tell the students is, "Ignore as much of this shit as you can." Either you're an actor or you're not an actor, and there's not a fucking thing you can do about it. Brando was great just by being Brando. If he was a dishwasher and he came out to bus your table, you'd watch him all the way back to the kitchen and be like, "What was *that*?"

In terms of acting *process,* you have a lot of really respected acting coaches and teachers, like the late Lee Strasberg, who really know their shit. They have some good ideas. But I think the way that acting classes can be best put to use is thinking of them as a place to work out. It's like if you're a musician and you've got nowhere to play, but somebody's willing to let you come to their little workshop singing group every other week and play your songs. Now you have a place to work out and do your shit. Maybe you won't get *better* at it, but you'll get more comfortable. Acting classes are invaluable in that sense.

So I go into Widlock's class the first time, and I sit in the back of the class, like I used to do in Maudie Treadway's acting class when I was sixteen. But now I'm actually watching all these actors going up there and doing scenes and monologues. The class is interesting enough that I come in a second time to watch for free, and this time, after class, I go up to Widlock to talk with him.

"Look," he says to me, "here's what you gotta do if you really want to join the class: either prepare a monologue or get someone from the class or whatever to prepare a scene with you and come back next week to do it. We'll see from there."

I knew I was being auditioned to see if he thought I was worthy of being in his class. It was like forty or fifty bucks a class, which to me was like $1.2 million, but I go back to my cousin's place in San Bernardino, and I tell Tom, "Yeah, they told me I gotta prepare a scene or a monologue, I don't know . . ."

Tom had all these Shakespeare books lying around. So I flip through *Othello* and suddenly think, *Oh, I know what I'll do!*

I always wrote short stories, and in high school acting class I would do lots of characters, so I made a plan to rewrite Shakespeare using regular language. And I'd play every character.

Othello's a good story, I think. *I know situations like that. I'll do that one.* So I start writing it down, but get lazy about twenty pages in and think, *Oh fuck it, I can make the rest of it up, I know this story.*

So I go back Wednesday night to the Crossroads of the World. John, as always, is sitting up on this little platform on the stage, and he goes, "Billy, you got something?" I say, "Yeah, I got something, it's a monologue or whatever." When it's my turn, I go up on the stage thinking I could do whatever the fuck I wanted because that's what he told me. "Whatever you want to do," he said, so that's what I did. I rewrote *Othello*. The play was now called *Othie and Desi,* after the main characters, Othello and Desdemona, and I did it from the point of view of Iago, the bad guy, from his jail cell after everything had gone down. I called him "I-A-Go the Redneck."

So I start by saying, "Look, my name's I-A-Go. I got in a lot of shit here a while back, and this is how it played out. There was a black dude named Othie, right? . . ." And that's the way I did it. I played Desi as this rich chick—her dad was this rich dude, you know, Romeo and Juliet–ish—and Cassio as this real foppish kind of gay dude. At the end, I-A-Go goes, "What the hell hath thou wrought upon this girl?" or something like that, and of course Othie turns around and says, "Hey, man, I killed a bitch, can't you see that?" I did all the different voices too.

John stops me after I had been going for about forty minutes. Everybody had just been sitting completely still during the performance, but after John stops me, they all start applauding like crazy. *Shit, I killed these motherfuckers, didn't I?* I think to myself. Then John jumps up on his perch and goes, "Wow, okay, first of all, right off the bat, I have to tell you when you do a scene or a monologue, it needs to be three to five minutes." And I go, "Oh, sorry, I didn't know that." Then he goes, "Second of all, I'm sorry I stopped you. How much more of this is there?" I tell him, and he goes, "Come back and finish this next week if you can squeeze it down a little. But from now on, three to five minutes."

Then he goes, "How did you feel?" which acting teachers ask, but I didn't know acting-teacher-speak yet, so I say, "I feel all right. I could use a cheeseburger, but other than that I'm all right, you know?" And he goes, "Did you feel you accomplished what you wanted to accomplish?" And I go, "Not yet, there's a lot of this shit left, I mean, like you said, I'm going to come back next week." And he says, "No, I mean, what you did here, do you feel like you accomplished something?" And I say, "Yeah, absolutely. I was just telling you a story, you know?" And he goes, "Amazing, amazing. Okay. We'll talk later. We gotta get on to some other people." So somebody else comes up, and they do their thing from *Forty Bales of Cotton* or whatever the hell it was.

After class Widlock comes up to me and says, "I didn't want to say this in front of everybody, but I've never had anybody in my class that does this kind of thing." I'm thinking back to Maudie Treadway when he adds, "I've had a lot of good actors in my class, but you've got some kind of *thing* here, you're very different. I think you should probably always stick to what you did tonight, which was original, something of your own invention. And I have a feeling that you need to write your own stuff, that you need to come up with your own characters. I don't think you're the kind of guy that needs to stand in the cattle call. You're going to make your career as a true original."

The class after he said all that stuff to me, I say, "John, I'd love to be in this class, but I don't have any money. I'm completely broke and rooming with my cousin in San Bernardino." He goes, "Don't worry about it. You'll either pay me back or you won't, but I think this is going to be worth it for me."

After that, I would take Tom's car every Wednesday into L.A., into Hollywood, to the Crossroads of the World on Cherokee and Sunset. John Widlock became like my keeper. In Hollywood, sometimes acting teachers become your protector and your psychologist.

John had this house over on Bronson Avenue up by the Hills that was pretty modest—a nice house, probably five or six rooms—but to me, his house was a mansion. He taught in San Francisco and L.A., so he'd go away for periods of time and would have me house-sit, which for me was this amazing luxury. He had cable television, and I watched Z Channel and I couldn't believe it. During that time of watching Z Channel, I got into watching foreign films and all these things that I'd never really watched before. There was all this great shit that would eventually come out of that. Today Widlock's a cattle rancher in Australia.

CHAPTER NINETEEN

Let's Don't Start No Circus

I N '81 OR '82, I JOINED A THEATER GROUP CALLED WEST COAST EN-semble, where I had the great opportunity to hang out with this guy Don Blakely, who introduced me to all these great character actors like Phil Peters, Jimmy Victor, and Rip Torn. The first thing Rip Torn ever said to me was, "They told me you were from Arkansas. I'm from Texas, and I don't like Arkansas for shit." And I said, "Well, nice to meet you too." Somehow through that bunch I also met Phil Bruns, a New York character actor. If you ever watched *Mary Hartman, Mary Hartman,* he played Mary Hartman's father, who on the series went crazy.

I had some great times in the West Coast Ensemble, which I was in from 1981 through about 1987 or 1988. I'm still friends with those people. I have a few friends who are leading actors. I consider Dennis Quaid and Bruce Willis good friends. I don't see Bill Paxton that much anymore, but we came up and spent most of our time running around together in the mid- to late eight-ies through the early nineties, and I talk to him every now and then. But the friends that I see on a regular basis are not famous guys. The guys I was in the theater group with are the ones that come over and hang out. A couple of those guys come over just to watch movies and talk about character actors. It's the *character*

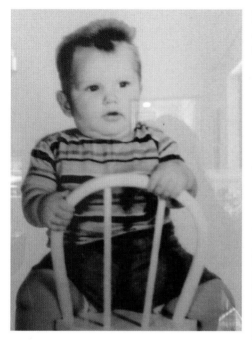

Fattest baby in Clark County, Arkansas. Thirty pounds at seven and a half months.

Jimmy's second birthday, Hatfield, Arkansas, 1960.

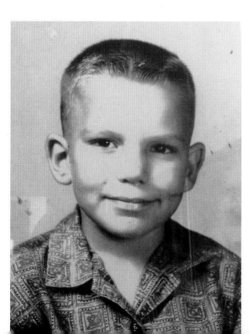

Second-grader in Mount Holly, Arkansas. Just being happy there's no Internet.

My dad, me, Jimmy, and little brother John David. Probably before or after church, 1968.

My grandparents, Claude David Faulkner and Maude May Faulkner.

Me and my brothers John David and Jimmy, Christmas 1975.

The band Hot 'Lanta in 1974 or '75. We weren't from Atlanta, but Arkansas was hot. "Hot 'Rkansas" didn't sound good.

Onstage around 1975 or '76 with our band Nothin' Doin'. That's old friend Mike Shipp on the left playing bass. I think this was Morrilton, Arkansas.

With old buddy Broderick Collins on a bridge somewhere. Looks like I'm holding something. Probably 1979 or '80, just before coming to L.A.

Karl Childers, with books and french-fried potaters. *Photograph by Michael Yarish. Courtesy of Miramax.*

With the late great J. T. Walsh. From *Sling Blade. Photograph by Michael Yarish. Courtesy of Miramax.*

With Billy Wilder at his office,
1996. Great director. Great man.

With June Carter Cash at the Carter
family home in Virginia.

Bridget Fonda, Bill
Paxton, and me on the
set of *A Simple Plan*.
Bridget didn't want
the watermelon to get
too cold. *Photograph
courtesy of Lynne
Eagan.*

In paradise with
Sam Raimi on
the set of *A
Simple Plan*.
*Photograph
courtesy of
Lynne Eagan.*

John Cusack and I on the set of *Pushing Tin*. Looks like a serious conversation. *Photograph courtesy of Lynne Eagan.*

Trout fishing in Canada. *Photograph courtesy of Lynne Eagan.*

With the Cards greats Mark McGwire and Bob Gibson. *Photograph by Jim Herren, St. Louis Cardinals.*

At Oceanway Studios in Nashville. Great time there doing demos in 2000 or so. Jim Cox and Jim Mitchell.

With Randy Scruggs in some airport. Probably Nashville 'cause we look depressed.

With the great Bruce Dern. We're pretending to be Dizzy Dean and Paul Dean. We have our own Gashouse Gang.

Holding Dan Lanois's bird in Silver Lake, California. Hey, not a bad song title.

With great drummer and pal Brady Blade and road crew Jim Mitchell, Micro, and Dirty Don in Stockholm, maybe 2000? *Photograph courtesy of Felicia Molinari.*

Visiting Eleanor Rigby's grave. *Photograph courtesy of Felicia Molinari.*

Shaved my head, went on tour, and acted like a tourist along the way. Strawberry Field, Liverpool. *Photograph courtesy of Felicia Molinari.*

Actually on "Ferry Cross the Mersey" with Gerry Marsden. *Photograph courtesy of Felicia Molinari.*

In the Cavern Club with Gerry Marsden, Liverpool. Now that's history! *Photograph courtesy of Felicia Molinari.*

Here's how it looks when a 140-pound guy with arms like noodles cuts sleeves off of an Irish rugby jersey. *Photograph courtesy of Felicia Molinari.*

No comment. *Photograph courtesy of Lynne Eagan.*

With John Prine on the set of *Daddy and Them*. This was moments before we got married. *Photograph courtesy of Lynne Eagan.*

With Patricia Arquette on the set of *The Badge*. *Photograph courtesy of Lynne Eagan.*

Lost in a field with Barry Levinson, one of my favorite directors. *Photograph by Richard Cartwright. Courtesy of MGM Media Licensing.*

On *Bandits*, somewhere on the Northern California coast. A rare peaceful moment in my noggin. *Photograph by Richard Cartwright. Courtesy of MGM Media Licensing.*

Bruce and I once again facing off on *Bandits*, fighting over Cate Blanchett. We both won. *Photograph by Richard Cartwright. Photograph courtesy of MGM Media Licensing.*

With my '67 Chevelle, Beverly Hills. 2001, I think.

Lynne Eagan, Kristin Scott, Joani Yarbrough: make-up, personal assistant, and hair stylist. Respectively, Lynne sixteen years of service, Kristin twelve years, and Joani fourteen years. *Photograph courtesy of Lynne Eagan.*

On the set of Travis Tritt's video "Modern Day Bonnie and Clyde." *Photograph courtesy of Lynne Eagan.*

Standing by a graveyard during *Monster's Ball. Photograph courtesy of Lynne Eagan.*

On the set of *Monster's Ball. Photograph courtesy of Lynne Eagan.*

This is either me on the set of *Levity,* or my friend Rickey Medlocke, guitarist for Lynyrd Skynyrd. *Photograph courtesy of Lynne Eagan.*

As Davey Crockett on the set of *The Alamo. Photograph courtesy of Lynne Eagan.*

In Austin moments after getting a REMEMBER THE ALAMO tattoo. Think I was also peeing on the floor.

Back when I was an astronaut. I think this was Mars … could've been Saturn … *Photograph courtesy of Lynne Eagan.*

With my longtime stunt double Mickey. Thank God for him. *Photograph courtesy of Lynne Eagan.*

Killed by The Rock. *Photograph courtesy of Lynne Eagan.*

actors that I always loved. The guys that made me want to be an actor are the guys who were down the line on the cast list usually.

These friends are still struggling—my age and still in acting classes. They actually have other jobs. But John Ford always had the same guys in movies, and I have a couple of guys like that I try to always get in my movies, even if it's not a movie I'm directing. Ritchie Montgomery from Natchez, Mississippi, is one of them. Cat Daddy, as we call him, was in *Monster's Ball* and *Jayne Mansfield's Car*—this movie we're working on now—and a couple of other things. Brent Briscoe is another. He's from *Sling Blade* and *A Simple Plan,* which was the part of his lifetime. I also cast him in *Jayne Mansfield's Car.* Those guys are really precious to me. As you know by now, *characters* are real precious to me.

I have a friend named J. P. Shellnutt who we put in *Jayne Mansfield's Car.* I admire him more than I do most people. He's just a guy from Americus, Georgia, who lives in Houston and used to be a car broker, but he's kind of a mythical creature. I met him through Billy Gibbons—I've known those guys from ZZ Top for more than thirty years, and they've always been real good to me. J.P. does security for us on the road—that's his job title anyway—but he's really just our hanging-out buddy. J.P. was sort of Gibbons's mascot for a long time—now he's mine, mainly. He's the kind of character I'm drawn to.

JIM VARNEY WAS A GOOD FRIEND AND ONE OF THE ALL-TIME GREAT character actors. He did all the "Vern" commercials and the Ernest movies, *Ernest Goes to Camp* and *Ernest Goes to Jail.* He ended up making a lot of money from it.

Varney grew up working in a tobacco barn. He's a descendant of the Hatfields and he and I tried to make the Hatfield and McCoy story for years. Nobody could quite get it. Varney had a DeLorean up on blocks in his yard—a DeLorean up on blocks, now *that's* a hillbilly—and with all the money he had, he still lived in a three-bedroom brick house in White House, Tennessee, which was Andrew Jackson's stopover place when he'd return to Nashville.

He even had a bumper sticker on the back of his sports car, which said, IT'S ME, IT'S ME, IT'S ERNEST T, you know, from *The Andy Griffith Show*. One time he came to pick me up in front of the Loews in Vanderbilt Plaza there in Nashville. The car park guys came out, and I said, "No, he's just picking me up." But then I saw Varney—who kept mouthwash in the middle of the console—opening his door and spitting the mouthwash right out by the car park guy. He was just that way.

He used to call me Elvis. One time he goes, "Hey, Elvis, I want to take you to a place that will blow your mind," and he took me to this strip joint that was in the middle of a dirt parking lot. You'd walk through this curtain, and there was a guy behind one of those windows where you pass the money underneath. Now, this was in the mideighties, before I was famous. I was an actor, and I was in shit, but I wasn't like Jim Varney. People in Nashville knew who he was. Anyway, we go in there, and he goes, "You're going to love this shit, Elvis, the chicks in here are hotter than hell." But this was in the middle of the day, and the two in the afternoon shift at a strip joint is usually not very good. I could see through the curtain, and it was just three drunks and a couple of old worn-out girls who had operation scars and shit.

So, I was just kind of standing there in the shadows when the guy behind the window goes, "Hey, man, wait a minute, are you who I think you are?" Varney puts our five bucks or whatever underneath the thing and goes, "Yeah, but let's don't start no circus."

Varney was a real cheap tipper, and he gave the guy a dollar to keep quiet. A dollar. I used to go behind Varney all the time because his tips rattled. We'd be at the Four Seasons and Varney would give them, like, fifty cents on a $300 bill, so I'd always go behind him and put some money down because it was embarrassing. But he was the greatest guy I ever knew in my life and a great actor who got pigeonholed as that Ernest character he created, but it was fantastic.

CHAPTER TWENTY

"When I Come Around"

I can't give up before I even try

I can't put on the clothes before I'm dry

If I'm strung out before I come unwound

Then I may end up coming back before I come around

—"When I Come Around" (Thornton/Andrew)

TOM AND I EVENTUALLY MOVED INTO A ONE-ROOM APARTMENT OVER on Motor Avenue that was a converted motel. Then I went to work for about a year and a half at Shakey's Pizza Parlor in Culver City, while Tom looked around for some kind of highbrowed work. He was under the impression that since he had been an English teacher back in Arkansas he was going to become an English teacher in California, until he found out that you have to take a whole other damn bunch of tests to be an English teacher in another state. Tom was smart and I was a dumb ass.

I have dyslexia and severe obsessive-compulsive disorder, so when I'm reading a book, I can't end a paragraph on the letters *th* or *d*. So when I finish a paragraph, I have to go back up and find a word that's soft and doesn't have any sharp edges on it or anything that ends in a *th*. Like a word that ends in an *f* is good, or a word that ends in a *b* is good, so I have to go back and read the sentence that ends in a *b* or an *f* and skip to the next paragraph without, even out of the corner of my eye, seeing the *th* or the *d* again. If I read things that are bad signs for my obsessive-compulsive disorder, I have to go to the previous page, reread it, and go to the bottom of the other page without looking at the rest of that page again before I go on. It can take me a month to read two pages. My obsessive-compulsive disorder is not "I put my left shoe on first," it's geometrical configurations in my head. I now figure out these things naturally, so you would never know that I'm doing all these things while we're talking. Besides, as we're talking, these are angles that are comfortable for me right now.

So you combine dyslexia with obsessive-compulsiveness and it gets to be some really complicated shit.

The point is, I'd never done anything except physical labor.

My first job was working in the grocery store that I lived by. I went in the morning or the afternoon, depending on when the guy wanted me out there at the ranch, stamping prices on cans and stocking the shelves. When I was done doing that, he sent me out to haul hay. That was a miserable fucking job. I also worked at a machine shop like out of a Charles Dickens book. *That* was also a miserable fucking job. I worked at a sawmill, which was a *dangerous* fucking job. I worked for the Arkansas Highway Department, Hot Spring County Road Department, where I drove a truck, shoveled asphalt, ran a backhoe, and hauled heavy equipment. I also worked as a carpenter and in a storm-door factory.

Anyway, sometimes I took Tom's car, sometimes I took the bus to Shakey's Pizza Parlor, where I made it all the way to assistant manager, which meant I was just kind of in charge of all these eighteen-year-olds. There was a manager, who was about my age—twenty-four or something—and we were the old guys. All the rest of them were kids. It was a pretty good job, though. It got us through.

I brought home $96 a week. We paid our $90 rent by the week for this one-room apartment with a bed and a bathroom—no kitchen or anything. It was just like the damn motel room that it *used to* be. Tom had a toaster oven, and we had one of those little bitty refrigerators about two feet tall, like you get in a mini-bar, but we didn't have any money so we didn't have anything to put in it anyway.

With the six dollars we had left over after rent, we'd buy a bottle of generic rum at Lucky Supermarket and a box of powdered doughnuts every Friday. You're wondering how we ate. Obviously a box of powdered doughnuts wasn't going to hold us over. Working at Shakey's, every day on your lunch break you made your own little eight-inch pizza. I knew Tom wouldn't have anything to eat until Friday, so every day, instead of eating lunch, I would make this damn personal pizza at the end of the night, and instead of just making a little pepperoni pizza, I stacked everything they had on there, cooked the shit out of it, and brought it home.

I would get home about one or two in the morning. Tom would go to sleep real early, so I'd wake him when I came in, and we'd get up and eat. At one or two in the morning, every night.

Nobody lived in this place that Tom and I lived in but probably dope addicts and stuff—and me and Tom. Tom had decided that since I was the junior partner of the team, I would sleep on the floor because we didn't want to sleep two guys on the same bed. I mean, *I* would have been happy to—I sleep on the corner anyway and I don't move when I sleep—but Tom had decided it would be better if he slept in the bed and I slept on the floor.

We were writing screenplays then, and on Friday nights we'd drink the rum, eat the powdered doughnuts, and talk into this voice recorder we used for writing our scripts. We started writing what was our second screenplay back then. It was called "Good Intentions," and it was never made.

There was this girl that was living in the building who got a crush on me. She got a *big* crush on me. She would kind of follow me around and stare at me. She wore a newsboy hat, jeans, a shirt, and tennis shoes, but she must have been in some type of bad accident because she was burned and horribly disfigured beyond recognition. I can't tell you how old she was, though she seemed to be maybe in her twenties or thirties, but she was literally melted. She had no nose, a hole for a mouth, and a very high-pitched voice. She had patches of hair, but it was mostly all burned off. She had no hands—she just had two sort of knobs there at the end of her arms, like pincers. Just horribly disfigured.

So I was in the shower one day, getting ready to go deep-sea fishing with Phil Bruns. See, Bruns told me, "If you ever want to go fishing sometime, you can go deep-sea fishing out at the marina, $17.50, and they give you the rod and reel, the bait, and they take you out on the boat for three hours. It's fun, and I'll pay for it because I know you're broke." This deep-sea fishing was for rock cod. You have five hooks on your line, you lower it to the bottom of the ocean out there, and five rock cods would hop onto it instantly, like fleas. Your limit is fifteen, and you catch your limit in like ten minutes. You can pay the guys there a couple of extra dollars and they'll fillet them for you, but I didn't do that. I brought them home, sawed their heads off, and cleaned them in the bathtub so that Tom and I could cook them in the toaster oven.

Anyway, I was taking a shower getting ready to go down to the marina to go fishing with Phil Bruns and somebody's banging on the door. Tom's not home, I had no idea who it was. I had really long hair then because, like I said, I had been a hippie musician back home and I hadn't caught on yet that if you were going to be an actor you had to get a haircut. So I got this wet hair hanging down, I got a towel on, I open the door, and it's her. Scared the shit out of me. She scared the shit out of me all the time when I saw her. Not any disrespect to her, it's just that I couldn't help it. If I open the door and there's a burned person like out of *House of Wax* there, I jump.

She asked me, "Can I have a picture of you?" and I said, "A picture of me? I dunno. What do you want that for?" "I want to be able to look at beauty like you," she says to me. And I go, because I got a little bit of an ego, I go, "Yeah, sure."

So I had two Polaroids, one was of me and Tom with a stripper in Nashville and the other one was some Polaroid of me sitting there somewhere like an idiot. So I give her this Polaroid, and she says, "Thank you," and she wants to know if I would come down to her room sometime, hang out with her and her roommate. Her roommate, who was a big, heavyset blond woman, used to get in fights with this dude in the middle of the street. Tom and I used to watch it out the window.

"Yeah, I'll get back to you on that."

Another time I was running across the street to use the pay phone—since we didn't have a phone, every now and then I would take one of my quarters and go to the Korean market on the corner where there was a pay phone and make a call to my mom back home—I turned the corner, and the melted woman was standing right there. I screamed, *"Goddammit!"* because it was like out of a horror movie. She started crying and—I'll never forget this because her face was like a road map of big, melty, waxy-looking stuff—the tears were going, like, *not* straight down. Now *that's* a great image, of these tears that had to go down these trails.

We ultimately found out—and I'm not sure how we found out, I think Tom found out—that it was a guy. The melted girl was a guy.

I wish now that I had just hung out with this cat and found out his story and his mentality, but I wasn't psychologically prepared to get involved in a friendship with him at the time. I wasn't grown up enough to see the beauty in it.

CHAPTER TWENTY-ONE

"Dead End Drive"

Some of us are broken from the very start
And we don't know how to fix ourselves
It seems, like me, you've been torn apart
There's a lot of us on the shelves
It's easy to escape through an open door
But the jail inside won't die
Feelin' claustrophobic and waitin' for
The exhale of a sigh

—"Dead End Drive" (Thornton/Andrew)

I DON'T REMEMBER THE FIRST TIME I EVER SAID ANYTHING PUBLICLY about these phobias I have. I don't know if you call them phobias exactly. I just get creeped out by stuff. I don't like real old things. I like modern. If I were given the opportunity to eat in an old English restaurant with old velvet drapes and castle-y-looking chairs, stone walls with mildew on them, or a bright spanking brand-new Japanese restaurant, I'll take the Japanese restaurant, that's just the way it goes with me.

I can't watch those *real* old-time movies while I'm eating, especially silent ones from the twenties, even the sound pictures from the early thirties, when they're about England, or Scotland, or France. If I see some big old gold carved ornate chair with a velvet cushion on it, I get spooked. It's just something about that time period. I would have weighed about twenty-five pounds if I lived back then, because I couldn't have eaten around any of that stuff. I can't ladle out some gravy while I'm looking at some big old fat king sitting in one of those chairs with all the cobwebs in the corner.

I have a fear of Benjamin Disraeli's hair. And I don't know if it's a *fear,* because I'm not worried that Benjamin Disraeli is going to show up one day and get me with his hair. It started when I saw this movie on Disraeli. I was broke at the time, and I was living in Arkansas in the house I grew up in. My mom had gotten remarried after my dad died and had moved to Louisville, Kentucky, with my younger brother. I was working for the county road department, and I lost my job in the winter. It was snowing, I didn't have any money, but every now and then my mother would send me ten or twenty dollars, whatever she could. My stepfather had money, he was a doctor, but he wouldn't give her any, and he sure as hell wouldn't send *me* any. I got the gas turned off after a while. I would sit in this old easy chair that was my dad's. It had holes in it by then. Somehow I had cable television even though I didn't have any money. I didn't pay for it, and they didn't know I had it. I think I paid to have it hooked up, but then I couldn't pay for the subscription and they left it on for some reason. This was around the time when cable television first came out.

Anyway, I was sitting in a freezing cold house wearing a coat. I slept in this easy chair every night in a big coat with a blanket on me. You could see your breath in the house, but I had cable TV. I'll never forget it. I walked about a mile and a half up to the store with the ten dollars my mother had sent me. It was freezing cold. I bought myself a Swanson TV dinner—a chicken dinner, which was my favorite—some Hostess Sno Balls, a Dr Pepper, and some Lance cheese crackers. At the time, having all this food was a thrill. I was going to make my TV dinner and I was going to watch me something good on cable TV.

I had no gas, but the oven worked because it was electric, so I put the TV dinner in the electric stove, cooked it all up, and sat down to watch something on TV. I was starving and about to eat my TV dinner when I switched channels and, just for a second, saw this guy, George Arliss, who was playing Disraeli. He had this big old weird face and teeth and that creepy wispy hair sticking back like Larry from the Three Stooges. And the set showed heavy drapes and those big old chairs and a stone-looking table. I couldn't eat my TV dinner just from seeing that. I switched the channel right off the bat and ended up watching a movie. Later on I was able to eat my TV dinner, but it was ruined at that point, because I had to reheat it. So that's how that whole Benjamin Disraeli thing started.

I also have a real live fear of Komodo dragons. People say, "Well, why would you be afraid of Komodo dragons, because what are the chances you're going to be walking down the street in Beverly Hills and run into a Komodo dragon?" I don't even want them in the world, that's the fact of the matter. One time a guy sent me a letter from some "save the animals" group—now I'm all for saving animals, but Komodo dragons are dinosaurs and they have no business here. They don't do a thing for anybody except kill things and eat them. And the way they kill—they recently discovered Komodo dragons actually have pockets of venom. They used to think that it was just the bacteria in their mouths that made them so poisonous, but now they know they have venom. They bite you and the poison starts to work and you go blind and start to lose your muscles. They'll sit there for however long it takes you to die, then circle around you and then they'll eat you. Well, that creeps me out. Why would we want them?

In the stories we read growing up, guys slay dragons. They don't have classic stories about a little boy getting his first dragon. (Well, except the song "Puff, the Magic Dragon.") They're dragons, you're supposed to kill them. They generally only exist on one island in the world, the island of Komodo, in the Indonesian Islands, and it's not like I want to go there, but they got one in the zoo here in San Francisco. Sharon Stone took her husband there for his birthday—apparently, he wanted to walk with the Komodo dragons. I understand swimming with the dolphins. I don't understand walking with the Komodo dragons, it doesn't make any sense to me. Sure enough, he got bit and ended up in the hospital. I just don't see any reason to have them on the planet.

I don't like to use real silverware, I never could. It doesn't feel good in my mouth, and I hate it when it hits my teeth. And it's too heavy. It's just too goddamn heavy. You know, I like things streamlined. I prefer plastic spoons and forks. At the same time, I'm all for getting rid of this big wad of plastic out in the Pacific Ocean. I'm a recycler. At the house we have plastic stuff for me, but it's the kind of stuff that's made out of corn and hemp and bamboo. We just don't use that regular plastic. I support not having plastic. I think people are too lazy these days. Just wash the dishes! I use everything else, real plates, real bowls, and the rest, but I prefer to use the phony forks and spoons.

I wish food and sleep weren't necessities, that they were just pleasures. I love food, the kind I have these days, but I wish you only ate for pleasure and it didn't put any weight on you and it didn't suck for your system or anything like that. I wish it were possible that if you don't want to eat for five days, you don't eat for five days, and when you do want to eat, you just eat. Just eat some fucking ice cream with hot fudge on it and not worry about any bad side effects to your health. I wish you didn't have to sleep and could stay up for three weeks and then one day think, *You know what I'd love to do today? I'd love to sleep.* Then just sleep for a week. Or three hours, or whatever you want. That's one of the things that really makes you think that there has to be some kind of intelligence behind this. That maybe we *are* just stardust, and it's this universe and the black holes and the big bangs and everything else, but that somehow, way back there somewhere, in the midst of all this, or in all of us or something, there's got to be some kind of spirit, some kind of *thing* that started us all, because otherwise why would Ding Dongs and butter and just *everything* be bad for you? That naturally fucking happened? Why is it that sex and food and drinking and smoking and all that kind of shit are bad for you? That seems like a rule to me. That doesn't seem like the natural order. It doesn't seem like evolution. It's just that that's the way our systems are. That all the good stuff is bad for you and all the stuff that tastes like cardboard and mud, *or* smells like ass and nutsack, those are the things that are good to eat. How can that be? You've got things to do, you want to stay up and have a party with your friends, you want to record for three days without stopping, but you've got to do this thing where you go to sleep and don't know shit and waste eight hours of your life. For eight hours of your life and you didn't know shit. If you want to know what's going on all the time, why not just be able to stay awake all the time? Somebody made a rule somewhere, that's all I'm saying. Somebody made a rule that the good shit is going to suck, and there are going to be a lot of people out there who really believe in this thing or person that made these rules, and they're going to judge people and talk bad about everybody who likes all those things that suck for you. Except for the food, by the way. I never met a real over-the-top, intense, churchgoing, fanatical-type religious person who didn't like food. Gluttony is supposed to be a sin, I've heard. Well, go to church sometime, there's a lot of sinners in there, believe me. So evidently, food is the one thing they don't mind breaking the rule on, the really religious people. It's just all the *other* fun stuff they judge you by.

There are certain phrases that get inside my skin. There are words that I can't hear or say. When I was young, we had Tastee Freez and Dairy Queen. They had a certain kind of fried potato item at these places called T-A-T-E-R T-O-T-S. I can't say the word, I have to spell it. It just bugs me that they'd name something that. I don't like it when they name food anything cute.

I went to a shrink a couple of times because whatever girl I was with at the time wanted to go to couples therapy. I found it to be horseshit, because you go to this person and all they're going to do is sit there and blame you for everything. All going to a therapist has ever done for me is get my ass chewed out by two people that day. So I never really did understand that. Well, you know the old saying: you split that word in half and it's "the rapist."

All that stuff seems normal to me, it doesn't seem weird. I think crazy people are people who don't know what they're doing. They have delusions. In other words, they're too crazy to function in life. I just don't like some things. I don't go bonkers and not know who I am, or start acting like a chicken. I just say I don't like creepy old castles. Which is not that weird. So if somebody thinks you're crazy because you don't like Benjamin Disraeli—I don't know, people have thoughts all the time that they just don't express. I make the mistake of saying them every now and then, that's the problem with me. I don't think van Gogh was crazy. Most people say, "He cut his ear off, that's insane!" No, the guy was so passionate over something that in the moment he went too far, but I don't think he was a crazy person, just intense.

"THE TOM EPPERSON STORY" BY TOM EPPERSON
(AS TOLD TO TOM EPPERSON)

Part VII

Obviously, we found a way to stay in Los Angeles. I could write a book about what happened to us over the next decade, but a few sentences will have to suffice for now. In visual terms, I see that period as a dark, turbulent cloud, with occasional flashes of beautiful golden light. It was a time of frustration, conflict, physical hunger, booze and parties, broken hearts and broken-down cars, life-threatening illnesses, deaths in the family, hopes raised and dashed . . .

CHAPTER TWENTY-TWO

"Was That My Only Ride?"

Surely this is a ghastly joke

Seems I was born but never awoke

Years have passed so the calendars say

It's hard to remember a given day

Did I really have my turn?

Did I really watch it burn?

Was that my only ride?

Did I sleep through it?

Did I lose my guide?

Before I knew it?

Was that my very best?

Did I just blow it?

Did I live in jest and never know it?

I can't believe it's been a waste

Can't I have just one more taste?

Will anybody cheer for more?

All I need is one encore

—"Was That My Only Ride?" (Thornton/Andrew)

As you can imagine, when Tom Epperson and I were first in L.A., we didn't have anything nice to wear. We had one jacket that we shared. It came from the only suit I ever owned.

When I was in my late teens, a friend of my mom's gave me her son's suit. I didn't have any money, my mom didn't have any money, and my dad was dead. It was a three-piece suit, green tweed, and it had a vest. I didn't bring the vest or the pants to California with us, I just brought the jacket, and when Tom and I had meetings, we would take turns wearing the jacket. Seriously, it was like, "I get to wear the jacket today."

There was one guy from my hometown who had ever been on-screen—movies *or* TV. He was on a pretty popular sitcom. This guy was a lot older than us, but I had gone to school with his sisters and got his number through them. Somehow we had managed to get an old answering machine that had a tape in it. You just had to push the button to listen to messages. Remember those? Anyway, one day we came home from some miserable shit, because every day was fucking horrible, and we had a message. It was this guy returning a bunch of messages we had left for him. Now, he wasn't like a big famous guy, but he was on a TV show, and to us he was, like, a big deal. "Sure, hometown boys," he said on his message, "I'll meet with you."

So we called him back and he was friendly. He said he wanted to meet us at Dan Tana's. At that time we didn't have a clue what Dan Tana's was. But we asked around a bit and learned that it was one of those places where a toothpick is $25. It was Tom's turn to wear the jacket.

We had to park down the road two blocks away because we couldn't just pull into the parking lot in Tom's shitty old Mustang that he never washed. It was light blue, but it had a coat of whatever the fuck he parked under on it, for years. You *couldn't* wash it because the paint would come right off—it was just glued onto it. Of course, it also had crap piled up in the backseat and was torn up everywhere.

Anyway, we went into Dan Tana's and stood at the bar—Tom wearing that lime-green tweed jacket and God knows what *I* had on—and ordered a beer or two. Spent all our money. That's the thing when you're broke. If somebody wants to meet with you, it's like, *I hope this son-of-a-bitch pays for it because otherwise I'm fucked.* We stayed at the bar for an hour or two waiting on this guy, and the staff kept getting on our asses at the bar for not doing anything.

"We're waiting on this guy, you know?" I said, trying to appeal to their better nature.

"Oh, okay, would you guys mind having a seat on the chairs we have right when you come in the door and quit hanging around at the bar?"

We waited on this guy forever, and he never showed up. This guy was, like, the seventh lead in a sitcom, but as I said, to us, in those days, if you had any connection with anybody, it was a huge fucking deal. This guy was the ticket. Because of this guy, we were going to make it. So, of course, we were devastated, just devastated. We trudged back to that piece-of-shit car with no fucking money, no ticket.

We got back to the house, and I don't know if it was the same day or the next day, but we got a message on the answering machine. "Hey, guys, I'm really sorry, I forgot I was supposed to meet with you guys, and I had to run down to San Diego." We just lit into his ass . . . cussing the answering machine at least. "Fuck you, cocksucker!" That kind of stuff. This guy was from our hometown, and we didn't understand how he could do this to us.

A little while later I remembered that the guy's sister sat in front of me in science class when we were in junior high and got her period right in front of me. It was, like, the first time she got her period, and she got shit all over the chair. Now, I didn't do this, but I wanted to call and leave him a little message: "By the way, I fucked your sister." Which I didn't, but I was going to say I did.

CHAPTER TWENTY-THREE

"Hey Joe Public"

I WROTE A SONG CALLED "HEY JOE PUBLIC" BY THE FACT THAT TIGER Woods went on television and apologized to me and you for messing around with those women. Tiger Woods doesn't owe anybody an apology except his wife and his kids. They're the only people he has to say anything to, but for some reason public apologies have become popular.

Whoever decided that if you want to sleep with somebody you got a disease? This goes for women the same as it does for men. I don't think, if my girlfriend messes around on me, that she's got a disease. I'd think she was an asshole for it, but she ain't got a disease. Sex addiction? I'm sorry, I just don't agree. You're horny. Maybe overly horny. But a goddamn disease? Leprosy is a disease. If you have any red spots on your face, or boils, or your nuts are falling off, your finger is falling off at the joint, you're so weak you can't get up out of the chair, *those* are diseases. Seeing some chick working at the car wash and deciding to get her phone number is not a disease.

And if somebody does think it's a disease, and if it is making people miserable, then God bless them, I feel bad for them. I'm not a scientist. But if Tiger Woods has to apologize to the world for his transgressions because he's a role model, then I can think of a whole lot of other athletes, preachers, movie producers, TV personalities, etc., who should do the same thing. There have been athletes that have committed armed robbery, sold dope, and worse. This world is out of control with its judgment of others and whatnot.

CHAPTER TWENTY-FOUR

"Never Been Dead in My Life"

People tell me I oughta slow down, on the chemicals and booze
But I've put everybody under the table, it seems I just can't lose
I don't take shit from a livin' soul, I sleep with a butcher knife
I've pissed on Mother Nature's shoes, but I've never been dead in my life
My friends all warn me
But luck adorns me
You see
Never been dead in my life
Never been dead in my life
Death has called me to his door
But I've never been dead in my life

—"Never Been Dead in My Life"
(Thornton/Andrew)

I NEARLY STARVED TO DEATH IN 1984. I WAS LIVING IN A SHITTY APART-ment in Glendale. I hadn't been there too long, it had just been painted, and I woke up on a Sunday morning with a pain in my right side—a pain in me that I can't even describe to you. It felt like a toothache in my chest—a real bad toothache where you can't sleep at night, right in my chest.

It lasted for three or four hours, and then it finally went away. I thought, *Goddamn, that wasn't fun.* I mean, it was bad. I didn't have a job, I had no money . . . The last thing I ate was a loaf of ground beef—they used to sell ground beef in plastic, like a loaf—and a bag of potatoes I bought from Lucky's Supermarket. I just drank tap water. I couldn't get any help from my mom because she didn't have any money and the guy she was married to wouldn't allow her to send me any of his. But in all fairness, I was never able to ask for shit. I just never wanted anybody to know. I had read a story about how when Errol Flynn was at his lowest point, *that's* when he wore his best suit and acted like he had money. Tom didn't have any money either, but he had more than I did, so he gave me a jar of pennies, nickels, and dimes before he went on a train to visit his mom back in Arkansas. He also left me his shitty old Mustang because I didn't have a car, and if it hadn't been for that car, I would never have made it to the hospital.

It was on a Sunday when the pain came on the first time. That following Wednesday night I got the same pain, only this time it was on my left side. This time it got so bad I didn't even know who I was. It was a pain that's indescribable, and it spread all the way to both arms, my shoulder blades, my whole back, my chest, everywhere.

For some reason, I thought if I could maintain contact with myself, I wouldn't die. *If I keep looking at myself in the mirror I won't die,* I thought to myself. But I was as white as a sheet and in a cold sweat, so I ended up getting in the car and going to the hospital.

It was a real busy night around the hospital, and the girl at the desk wouldn't admit me to the emergency room there because I didn't have any insurance, I didn't have a credit card, and I didn't have any money. But this intern, a woman—I'll never forget her face, though I can't tell you her name—came up to the girl at the desk, which was a setup like a little booth, kind of like paying two dollars to go to the movies, and said, "What's the problem here?" I started something that resembled talking, but I could barely speak. This thing took my breath away. I felt solid, like the inside of me was full of modeling clay, and I couldn't breathe the pain was so intense. You know when you hear a kid crying and it's kind of broken up? That's the way I was talking.

The intern chewed the girl out for a second or two because when somebody has chest pains, you're supposed to let them in. She brought me in and put me behind a curtain. They had me lie down and gave me morphine. The curtain was probably a foot or two open—they didn't shut it all the way—and I saw some things that were not cool. The guy next to me—I saw his face for a second because his curtain wasn't shut all the way either, and I heard people talking. I later learned that the guy was in his twenties and a steering wheel had crushed him in a car wreck. He died within the first half an hour that I was there. They also brought in a black guy on a gurney who had been shot in the stomach.

They were going to ship me over to County because I didn't have insurance, but the doctor on duty that night—I'll never forget this guy as long as I live—looked at my medical records, saw that I was from Arkansas, and made them admit me to a room. Turned out he was a gastroenterologist from the Ozarks. It was just one of those connections.

They gave me so much morphine and Demerol it knocked me out, and I woke up the next afternoon. When I woke up, the pain was exactly like it was when I went in. But I remember a big fat dude that was a nurse on the floor—he was real funny, like John Candy. "You've been through quite a thing, huh?" he said.

They never determined what I had, but they put "probable viral myocarditis" on my records. That's when you get an inflammation of the heart muscle. Bob Dylan had something called pericarditis, which is different—myocarditis is an inflammation of the heart muscle, whereas pericarditis is an inflammation of the sac around the heart—but they feel very similar, supposedly, so when Dylan had his heart problem, I felt I knew exactly what the fuck he was going through. Really not good.

My mom told me they thought I had a heart attack, but I didn't have a heart attack. I wasn't any kind of candidate for a heart attack. I've never had any cholesterol or plaque issues. What it was was I was starving to death. Same thing that happens to anybody who doesn't eat. I had no potassium, no electrolytes, I had none of that shit.

I'd sit in my hospital room watching TV at two o'clock in the morning because I'm an insomniac and the fat guy who looked like John Candy would come and sit and talk to me. We were talking one night about food, and I told him my favorite thing in the world is butterscotch milkshakes. After that, while all these other patients got their three meals a day or whatever it was, he would bring me a butterscotch milkshake and a turkey and Swiss sandwich at one or two in the morning. He'd say, "Now don't tell anybody I'm bringing you shit because I'm not the dietitian." But he knew what was wrong with me, how I hadn't eaten in a really long time. He was a big dude, and he understood things like wanting to eat.

There was this cardiologist who was a real prick. Seemed that all he could think about was getting me the fuck out of there and over to the county hospital where all the other street people were. One day I'm sitting up, eating hospital Salisbury steak and mashed potatoes like a fucking crow because I'm starving, and this doctor comes in and says, "Well, I guess you're pretty happy. You *must* be pretty happy. You got free room and board and a nice meal." I knew right then that this was the wrong cat to put in charge of me. But then this doctor that admitted me, Dr. Dwyer—the Ozark guy—came around to see me. He was a really cool cat. He wanted me to stay until I was okay. I saw him over the years but lost touch with him. I wish I knew where some of these fucking people who helped me were because I would give them a television set or something.

They ultimately did ship me over to the county hospital, where I got to stay because our buddy Coby put his credit card down. It looked like something out of *Gone with the Wind,* all these people in one room. There were probably ten or twelve people in that room with me, and there were all these intern doctors talking about what an amazing case I was because I was so young and it was a cardio-far-whatever they called it. *These motherfuckers are going to experiment on me,* I thought. *I'm going to become a fucking laboratory rat here.* So after two or three nights there I found my pants and my shoes, but I couldn't find my shirt—and called Coby collect from a pay phone.

Coby came to pick me up in his truck, and I never went back. I was fine for all those years until I starved myself on purpose in 2000 and went back in the hospital for the same thing.

CHAPTER TWENTY-FIVE

"The Walking Extinct"

We are the walking extinct
Stumblin' over the bones of memories
We're the invisible link
Waiting and hoping that someone will see
We are the walking extinct
Watching the fossils fall and break apart
We're an ark about to sink
Drowning all the magic in our hearts
And it happened so slow
You'll never know what didn't hit you

—"The Walking Extinct" (Thornton/Andrew)

WHEN I WAS IN GLENDALE RECUPERATING FROM THIS SHIT, I TRIED to get social services to help me. I tried to get food stamps and whatever, but they needed so much shit from me, so much information, and I didn't know how to give it to them. I didn't have the proper paperwork or tax shit, and I couldn't remember my social security number, so I never got any of the stuff I needed. I was like, "Goddammit, I'm a fucking American, why can't you help me?"

But things started getting a little better when I got a job for a time. I also had a girlfriend then who kind of felt sorry for me, so she helped me pay for stuff. So I thought, *I better start doing some physical activity and eating right,* and I joined the YMCA in Glendale. The Glendale YMCA is a nice YMCA, not some shithole, and they had a world-class basketball gym, and since the job I had was kind of spotty—off and on—I could get to the YMCA to shoot hoops most days at seven A.M., when all the regular people were getting ready for work.

There were just a bunch of old men in the locker room when I was changing into my short britches at seven in the morning. I don't know how old they were then, but it was 1984 and they were World War II veterans, so you figure if the war ended in 1945, that would probably put them in their late sixties *then*. At the time I thought they were ancient. I would talk to these guys, and a couple of them would come out and shoot free throws with me. Turns out three or four of them were B-17 crew guys during World War II. One guy was a pilot, couple of guys were ball turret gunners, one guy was a tail gunner. Then there was a navigator, an engineer, a sergeant, who was a top turret gunner. I got to love these guys because I've had this thing for the B-17 bomber ever since I was a little kid.

MY GRANDMOTHER WAS A WRITER AND A SCHOOLTEACHER, AND AT her house where I was growing up in Alpine she had bookshelves all around the walls. Out of all those books she had, I'd just sit and stare at this book that was kind of blue-gray, but I never took it out. I'd just sit there and stare at it. This was before I could read. Then one day, when I was about nine, after I could read, I pulled it out of the shelf and opened it up. It had all these guys' pictures, and down there beside the pictures there was a little thing about each one like they have in a high school yearbook. Turned out they were all guys in Clark County who served in World War II. Next to their pictures it would say PFC So-and-So, killed in action May 15, 1942, or whatever, who their parents were, and whatever else. There were two guys in particular that I would stare at all the time. One's name was Olen G. Allison, and the other guy's name I don't recall. Olen G. Allison was a real skinny-looking guy. He had on the regular dress-looking hat tilted to the side, like they had in the old days. The other guy was kind of handsome, looked like a movie star, and in his picture he wore a leather jacket, a white scarf, and the leather flier's cap. They were both killed in action in World War II. Out of everyone in that book, I would sit for hours and I'd read their things over and over.

I was also drawn to these pictures of B-17 airplanes. Now, I don't believe in a fucking thing, practically—though of course we talked about my mother who has ESP, and I'm telling you she's told me shit that only exists in my head—but when I started reading about these B-17s, I was reading about something that I *knew*.

When I first met Coby, it must have been in 1981, he and I went out to the Chino Air Museum because I'd always had this thing for World War II airplanes, and they had a B-17 out there you could walk around in it. I went in from under the hull, crawled up the little steps, and walked straight to the front of the airplane. Now, if you didn't know a thing about an airplane and you wanted to know where the bombardier was, you'd probably look all over the place, but—and I had never physically been in a B-17—I walked past the waist gunner's position, straight past the navigator in the middle there, down beneath the cockpit into the nose of that thing, sat at the bombsight, and felt like I was home. After that I was convinced that I was a bombardier in a B-17 airplane in World War II. Now, it can be complete horseshit and explained by the fact that I just liked airplanes and my particular brain chemistry led me to that or some shit, but why did I pull that book out from that shelf and why did I stare at those guys all the time? And how did I know where every position was before I ever went in a B-17? Maybe there's a perfectly good scientific explanation for that shit. People get struck by lightning and they start playing Beethoven. All I know is, I knew shit that I didn't know.

Anyway, when I met these guys at the YMCA, I stuck to them like glue. I was obsessed with them. I went to their meetings and became fast friends with a bunch of guys who were about seventy years old. I became real good friends with one guy, who at this time was a schoolteacher in Long Beach, who had been a ball turret gunner. He would come over to my apartment, and we would sit and talk for hours and hours. He even gave me some books to read. I'd planned on making this movie about B-17 bomber crews, because they have stories that would blow people's minds, but they already made one over at Columbia called *Memphis Belle*.

I even started going to their veterans' meetings down in Southgate/Downey and to a lot of Confederate Air Force events.

They made me an honorary member of the 94th Bomb Group, and I got their newsletter up until just a few years ago. I guess most of those guys I knew are long gone by now, but they were great guys.

CHAPTER TWENTY-SIX

To Billy Bob, from a Big Fan—Billy Wilder

I knew that I could make it, I knew the sky would clear
The boulevard would dry a spot and my star would appear
Shining on the footprints standing near
When you've reached the top
And the gold's rubbed off the chrome
There's no way to get back home

—"Every Time It Rains" (Thornton/Andrew)

COMING UP, I HAD NOTHING, YET I ALWAYS THOUGHT I HAD A SHOT. I always somehow accomplished the things I set out to accomplish, even on a small scale, so I didn't really think that you couldn't do shit. I got in a band that had regional success. I played baseball and became a very good pitcher. Part of it was ignorance—the fact that I didn't know any better—but whatever the case, I had belief in my ability. I never had belief in big success, but I had belief in moderate success. I never thought I was going to be a movie star, but I always thought, *I'm good enough that I'm going to have a career.* I thought I was going to be one of those guys you'd see in the old movies who was, like, the fifth guy from the left—that's who I thought I was going to be. I thought I *might be* Harry Dean Stanton. Shit, when Jeb Rosebrook, the guy who wrote *Junior Bonner* and produced the TV show I was on, *The Outsiders,* said, "You know who you are? You're Warren Oates," I was like, "Wow, what a compliment!" I never knew I'd become a movie star. When I started acting, my goal was to become a great character actor. That's all I ever thought I would be, or ever wanted to be. The other stuff just happened.

When I was twenty-nine, broke, and getting close to my first Saturn return, if you follow astrology, there was a fourth thing in this spooky through line that ran through my early days: Maudie Treadway at sixteen; Teddy Wilburn at twenty-four; John Widlock at twenty-five. And at thirty, it was Billy Wilder.

A friend of mine was working for one of these catering companies that do big parties for rich folks. I needed a job, so this guy asked if I could come work for a Christmas Eve party in Bel Air. I had worked in restaurants, but I only washed dishes, made pizzas, and stocked the salad bar. I tended bar at Shakey's, but all they had was beer and wine, so I didn't even know how to make a fucking drink. "I *can't* be a waiter," I said.

He said, "Look, do you have a tuxedo?" I said, "Do I have a tuxedo? No, I don't have a fucking tuxedo." So he gave me a tuxedo. He was like six-four, and I had to pin the sleeves and the pants up on this thing, but I drove over to Stone Canyon Road to be a waiter for a rich person's party on Christmas Eve.

I get there and they put me in charge of passing around little fish-head hors d'oeuvres and shit. Doesn't take me long to notice that Debbie Reynolds is over there, Dan Aykroyd and his wife, Donna Dixon, are over there, Dudley Moore is playing the piano, and there's Sammy Cahn, the old songwriter, talking to some little old short dude with a German accent. I didn't know who the dude was, but he was in good company.

Turns out it's Stanley Donen's party. Stanley Donen directed *Singin' in the Rain, Seven Brides for Seven Brothers,* all big MGM musicals. I finally got to eat at Dan Tana's one night with a guy who wanted Tom and me to write a screenplay, and I thought, *Wow, I hit the big time!* because I ate at Dan Tana's, and here I am passing out fucking hors d'oeuvres at Stanley Donen's house.

While I was passing out the fish heads, I went over by this fireplace thing and started talking to the little old German cat. He and some guy were talking about the old days, saying stuff like, "Yeah, I'll never forget, I was with Jimmy Durante . . ." when the German guy says to me, "So you wanna be an actor?" I wasn't clued in yet to how actors are waiters and I thought he had ESP, so I said, "Yeah, I do, I do want to be an actor, how did you know that?" And he goes, "Well, all you guys want to be actors. Here's the thing. You're never gonna make it." And I go, "Well, jeez, thanks a lot, thanks a lot." He says, "You know, you're too handsome to be a character actor and too ugly to be a movie star." I say, "Well, what can I do then?" And he says, "Well, can you write?" And I say, "Yeah, actually, I got a few screenplays." He says, "Actors are a dime a dozen in this place. They need good writers. So write your own stuff and create *your own* characters."

Then the boss guy comes over and chews my ass out for talking to one of the guests, and the little German guy tells him to go somewhere else. "I'm talking to this guy," he says. The boss guy walks away, and the German guy goes, "Look, writing is a real honest profession in a lot of ways. Some writers are full of it, but the great thing about them, even when they're writing stuff that is a bunch of shit, is they're interesting." Then he goes, "You got a life that's been interesting?"

"Yeah, it's been interesting so far."

"Well, write about it. Write about your interesting life, and maybe one of these days somebody else might think it's interesting too, and if you still want to be an actor, maybe you can be in whatever it is. If somebody buys it anyway."

This cat is really funny and really nice to me. I don't feel like a waiter with this guy. So I go back up to refill my little tray of fried fish heads, and one of these actor types who's working at the bar says, "What'd he say to you?" And I say, "Who?" and he says, "Billy Wilder." I say, "Billy Wilder?" And he says, "That little guy you were talking to over there, that's Billy Wilder." And I go, "The guy who directed Jack Lemmon and those cats?" He's like, "Yeah." And I'm like, "Well, if I had known that I would've probably left and not said anything to him." Once again, my ignorance gives way for me to not just pack it up. I'm not including everything Mr. Wilder said, but it changed my life in so many ways.

After that I started writing Karl and doing a one-man show at the theater where I did all my own characters, wrote all my own shit. I was later discovered out of the theater by casting director Fred Roos, who I owe and admire forever.

YEARS LATER, AFTER I'D DONE *SLING BLADE* AND BECOME AN OVER-night deal or whatever, I got a call from Billy Wilder saying he wanted me to have lunch with him in his office, right down here on Beverly Drive. I had just been nominated for two Academy Awards for the movie, and now Billy Wilder wanted to have lunch with me. So he gets me down to his office, and he orders sandwiches from Nate and Al's Deli, and he and I have sandwiches. From Nate and Al's. In Billy Wilder's office.

I'm sitting there having a turkey sandwich—with Billy Wilder—and he says, "So, I read this interview you did where it talked about how I had given you advice and how I was so nice to you when you were a waiter. This thing, it really moved me." That's why he called me down there. He had seen this interview with me saying this about him. Then he goes, "I don't remember a fucking bit about that, but it's a great story, and I'm glad I was able to give you some helpful advice." And he reminds me again, "I don't remember you from Adam, of course." And I say, "Yeah, that's okay."

Then he says, "I've got a book I want to sign for you," and he pulls a copy of the *Sling Blade* book of the screenplay out of his bookshelf. He signs it to me, "To Billy Bob, from a big fan— Billy Wilder." That was pretty wild.

Two directors were very nice to me. He was one, and then there was Stanley Kramer. The house I live in now was actually Stanley Kramer's house in the late fifties, early sixties, when he made *It's a Mad Mad Mad Mad World* and all those movies. Kramer took me under his wing, and to this day I'm good friends with his daughters and his widow. Stanley was a great man. Mr. Wilder was a great man. They both gave me hope and the benefit of their wisdom.

CHAPTER TWENTY-SEVEN

October 3, 1988

Who knows what makes a heart race too fast

And who knows what makes it stop

Somehow I still feel it was a mistake

Surely it wasn't just your heartbreak

And maybe the sky was just running out of hope

And maybe the heavens opened up and dropped down a rope

And you grabbed it

My brother

My brother

My brother

—"Fast Hearts" (Thornton/Mitchell)

TOM AND I WROTE A LOT OF STUFF THAT NEVER GOT MADE. WE SOLD our first screenplay to David Geffen in 1985 or 1986. Then we made a three-picture deal with Disney, with Touchstone. I was getting bits and pieces here and there, making a little money as an actor doing *Matlock* and some other TV work. I was never one to say that movie acting is better than TV acting. The only difference is that you have to move so fast in TV you don't have much time to work on anything. You can take all day to do ten lines in a movie. I hate it when people say, "Oh, he's a TV actor." There's some good stuff on TV. James Garner in *The Rockford Files,* he was terrific. Nowadays, *Curb Your Enthusiasm* makes me laugh, it's hysterical to me. J. B. Smoove as Leon, Larry David's roommate on the show, he's funny as shit. Jeff Garlin, all those guys. Larry David is one of the guys on my list that I want to meet. Maybe I'll regret it, you never know. You don't know until you meet somebody.

I know the Farrelly brothers pretty well, and they were shooting in Atlanta when we were making *Jayne Mansfield's Car.* They invited me over to their set one day when I was off. They said that Larry David had just left, because he's in the movie they were shooting. I just sat around on the set that day, so disappointed that I didn't get to meet him. You know, you can't ever stop being a fan. That's the most important thing for an artist. Never stop being a fan. It doesn't matter how big you get, you got to always be a fan. Once your ego takes over and you start hating other artists, that's when you'll die inside. Like *somebody.* It doesn't matter who it is—it could be someone or some*thing* from forty years ago—but being a fan keeps you alive as an artist. It inspires you. Even though I'm in the entertainment business, I'm still a big fan. I love movies and music.

In 1987 I worked on a series called *The Outsiders* based on S. E. Hinton's book and the movie that was on Fox when Fox was a very new network. The show lasted a year, but it was the first time I made steady money as an actor. I was living with my buddy Coby and his wife, Katja, over in Glendale, I was seeing a bunch of girls, and I hadn't been this relaxed and had this much fun since I worked for the Arkansas Highway Department.

IF I COULD GO BACK TO ANY TIME IN MY LIFE AND RELIVE IT, IT WOULD be when I was making *The Alamo, Bad Santa,* or when I worked for the Arkansas Highway Department back in 1979, right before I came back to California. I worked for the highway department for about a year and a half, driving dump trucks, shoveling asphalt, and salting the roads when it snowed or iced over. I was one of the guys that took the tractor and the bush hog and mowed the median and the banks. I drove a patch truck and patched holes in the road. A good friend of mine named Broderick Collins was my roommate during this time. He also worked at the highway department. It was just a good time when there was no responsibility. We didn't have a lot of money, but it was ours.

My mom had gotten remarried and moved off to Louisville, Kentucky, so we lived in the house that I grew up in, just me and Broderick. We'd get up at five-thirty in the morning and go to work at the highway department. When we got out at night, Broderick and I would get in his Firebird—which was like the one Burt Reynolds had in *Smokey and the Bandit*—put our good clothes on, and go to Hot Springs to just tear shit up. I had a couple of girlfriends over there. We'd work our asses off for the highway department all day and then fuck around all night.

I WAS HAPPIER THAN I HAD EVER BEEN FROM 1987 THROUGH OCTOBER 3, 1988, the day my brother Jimmy died. He was thirty years old. He had a virus at the time, but he would never go to the doctor and it got in his heart. They think he probably had rheumatic fever when he was a kid and they never caught it.

I was devastated. Me and my brother were real close. He was a genius. Jimmy was two and a half years younger than me, but he was kind of like the big brother because he was a lot more responsible. We grew up listening to Captain Beefheart and the Mothers of Invention together, and he was a brilliant songwriter in his own right. There are these people who there are only one of, and there was only one of my brother. I really admired him.

There are parts of my sense of humor and my vibe that died with him because, though he was a lot smarter and a lot more talented than I am, he was the only person on the planet who understood certain things the way I did.

Jimmy was dark and moody. He was always to himself and quiet. We used to get in fights all the time. I was stronger than him, but I used to let him get the best of me in fights because I didn't want to hurt him. One time I held him down in the backyard—it was about a half-hour before my dad got home—and I had to keep holding him down because he wouldn't quit. I had to tell him, "If I let you up, do you promise you'll quit fighting me?" And he said, "No! Fuck you! If you let me up, I'll kill you, you cocksucker!" That's the way he was. He had a really bad temper. Jimmy would spit and yell and scream, hit you in the mouth, you'd be bleeding on him. He swung his fist like a windmill. He was a tough kid. A real *talented* kid. Great musician and songwriter. And he was real different. Jimmy was moody and very intense, sometimes aggressively nuts. He went to chef's school and became a pastry chef—he was a great cook. He turned me on to certain people in the eighties that I didn't know much about, like the BoDeans and Jason and the Scorchers. He was a very bright kid. He grew up to be a long-haired hippie like me. We were very close.

Jimmy died when he was thirty. I went crazy. I had a lot of the "why him, not me" thing. I think a lot of people have that, and I've never been completely happy since. Jimmy died before he could really show what he was, but we've recorded a couple of his songs, and I plan on doing some more. I still think I ought to call him and tell him when something happens and forget that he's been dead since 1988.

"THE TOM EPPERSON STORY" BY TOM EPPERSON
(AS TOLD TO TOM EPPERSON)

Part VIII

The phone rang. It was Mary Cross, mine and Billy Bob's agent. Billy happened to be at my grungy apartment, and as I listened to Mary I looked suddenly at Billy and gave him a thumbs-up. She had great news! We had sold our first script!

Billy and I, naturally, were euphoric. I lived in East Hollywood in a mostly Hispanic neighborhood on New Hampshire Avenue, and Billy and I walked around the corner to a Korean grocery and liquor store on Vermont. We bought a bottle of cheap scotch. We passed the scotch back and forth, drinking straight from the bottle, till it was empty. I woke up the next morning with the happiest hangover I've ever had.

It was February 1987, nearly six years after Billy and I had come out from Arkansas to make it in Hollywood. The script we'd sold, "Hands of Another," was a thriller about a homicide detective and an actor. We wrote it with the help of a real homicide detective who was working for the LAPD. We got $25,000 for an option and a rewrite. The most I'd ever earned in a year before that was $8,000, so this seemed like a fortune. I quit my part-time temp job—I'd been catching a bus downtown (since my car's radiator was shot and I couldn't drive it for more than ten minutes without it overheating) for the last fourteen months to work in the Population Research Section of the Regional Planning Department of the County of Los Angeles (yes, it was as tedious as it sounds)—and I moved to a new apartment, in Hollywood, north of Franklin, on the prettily named Primrose Avenue.

"Hands of Another," alas, never got made. A Michael J.

Fox movie with a similar plotline came along and blew us out of the water. But besides providing Billy and me with our first success, "Hands of Another" also led directly to our next project. Since we'd sold one cop script, we decided it would be smart to write another cop script, and with the help of our homicide detective friend, we immediately did so.

We called it "Color Me Bad." It was about a naive small-town chief of police in Arkansas who has a showdown with some vicious killers from L.A. Our agent Mary loved it, and within days of her sending it out Billy and I got another electrifying phone call: Tri-Star had flipped for "Color Me Bad" and wanted to buy it!

Well, Billy and I were in high cotton now. We'd sold two spec scripts in a row. We were finally beginning to tear Hollywood apart, just like we'd planned it. I flew back to Arkansas in triumph. It was only the second time I'd been home since Billy and I had left years ago. It was the middle of the summer, and I had a pleasant time playing tennis and working on my tan. The day before I was to go back to L.A., my mother convened a kind of family reunion to celebrate my success. She was one of nine children, so there were lots of people there. Cousins congratulated me, aunts kissed me, uncles slapped me on the back. And then the phone rang.

It was Billy, calling from California. His voice sounded terrible, and I asked him what was wrong. He said Mary Cross had just called. It seemed that our script had come to the attention of the president of Tri-Star; he'd read it, hadn't liked it, and had called the deal off.

I took my mother aside and told her what had happened. She was as shocked as I was. She asked me not to tell anyone because if I did it would ruin the reunion. So I and all my cousins and aunts and uncles continued to celebrate my nonexistent success.

The bad news cast a pall over the short remainder of my visit. It turned out that was the last time I was ever to see my mother. She dropped dead while taking a walk a few months later.

The initial flurry of excitement over "Color Me Bad" quickly died away, and now it was just another script floating around Hollywood looking for a home. One major producer said he'd take it on if, in the role of the white police chief, we agreed to cast Danny Glover. When we gently pointed out that Danny Glover was black, he said, what difference did that make? Well, since a central part of the story was the police chief having to confront his own racism, it made a difference to us, so we moved on. Then a major independent company said they'd make "Hurricane" (as we were now calling it) if we agreed to partner up with a certain hot young director. When we met with the director, he was such a flaming asshole that the whole project fell apart within an hour. And so it went for the next three years, till we met a producer named Ben Myron. We optioned the script to Ben for a dollar at a Hank Williams Jr. concert, then Ben and his partner, Jesse Beaton, took it to RCA Columbia, a video company that at the time was funding a lot of low-budget indie movies (including *Sex, Lies, and Videotape*). Larry Estes, head of the company, liked the script. It was shot in the fall of 1990 in L.A. and Arkansas under yet another title, "One False Move."

It starred Bill Paxton as a naive small-town Arkansas chief of police who has a deadly showdown with some hard-boiled criminals from L.A. Billy played one of the bad guys.

Unfortunately, we couldn't find a distributor for it. It sat on the shelf for a year and seemed to be headed straight to video. It was a rotten time. Billy and I hadn't had a writing job in a long while, and I was totally broke. My car was in hock to the Writers Guild Credit Union, and I was having to borrow money from a girl I'd recently met to pay the rent. And then the luck happened.

Movie critics Roger Ebert and the late Gene Siskel saw *One False Move* at separate film festivals in early 1992. Both went bananas over it and made it their personal campaign to see that the movie was released in theaters. It came out in May to rave reviews. It took us four years to get an agent, six years to sell a script, ten years to get a movie made, but Billy and I suddenly became a hot writing team, and Billy's acting career began to flourish. In their end-of-the-year show, Ebert named *One False Move* the second-best movie of the year while Siskel had it number one. Billy and I owe a big debt to the thumbs-up/thumbs-down guys.

CHAPTER TWENTY-EIGHT

Burt Reynolds Prophecy

I NEVER DID MUCH TV, BUT I DID WORK FOR HARRY THOMASON AND Linda Bloodworth-Thomason, who did *Designing Women* and *Evening Shade* with Burt Reynolds. In 1989, when they first started doing the Burt Reynolds show, *Evening Shade,* there was this casting director who was always really good to me. Her name was Fran Bascom. I was living in Glendale, sleeping on a blow-up mattress on the floor at my friend's house, when Fran called me one morning at, like, eight-thirty. She said, "Can you be at CBS over in the Valley at ten? They need somebody to play a florist in this pilot for this new Burt Reynolds sitcom."

Years ago, before I was ever thinking about being an actor, my mom told me that one of these days Burt Reynolds was going to be "instrumental" in my life. I'm like, *What the fuck does that mean?* She didn't know. I thought that maybe Mom's psychic abilities were off the mark on this one.

Anyway, Fran Bascom said, "They need somebody to audition, and I think you're going to get this, you just need to meet with the director. But I'm going to need you to get over there *now*." I said, "Yeah, okay." So I hauled ass over to Harry Thomason's office, where I met with the director for the episode, who happened to be Charles Nelson Reilly. I talked to him for a couple of minutes, and he said, "There are, like, seven, eight, maybe ten lines at the most." Then he read the lines with me. I went in thinking, *I'm the last son-of-a-bitch in the world they need to be a florist,* but what they were really looking for was a flower delivery boy. That made more sense to me. In fact, after we were done reading lines and he said, "You've got a job!" in that way Charles Nelson Reilly used to talk, I went over to the wardrobe people, who just kind of looked at me and said, "Yeah, what you're wearing is good."

I got on the set that night and looked around. Sitting up in the stands for the rehearsal, I saw Dom DeLuise, Doug McClure, and Rip Taylor. Then I saw Ossie Davis, Ann Wedgeworth, Elizabeth Ashley, Hal Holbrook, Charles Durning, Burt Reynolds, Marilu Henner, and all these people. I thought, *Shit, Burt Reynolds brought all his pals out to see the show.* I didn't know they were all *in* it. I was just thrilled being around all those guys. I was always a fan of character actors, and here on this set were a bunch of the best ones. I'm like, *This is high-dollar shit here.*

That night we shot the show in front of a live audience. My scene was with Burt. The scene was about the father's grave or something like that, it wasn't funny. More of a functional scene, really. So I went up on the porch, Burt came to the door, I handed off the flowers, said my lines the only way I knew how—which was to just say them—then I came off the stage to see Hal Holbrook standing there.

"Son, come here a minute," he said, "I want to talk to you." I thought, *Oh great. I fucked up and Hal Holbrook is mad at me.* But he calls me around the corner—they're still shooting while this is going on—and he whispers to me, "Son, let me tell you something. I've been an actor for forty-eight years (or whatever), and that was one of the finest, most natural pieces of acting that

I've ever seen in my lifetime, right there." My knees were shaking and shit. Hal Holbrook was fucking Mark Twain, *Jesus!* I was like, "Thank you, sir." All he said was, "I know you only did eight lines here, but I think you got something," and with that, Hal Holbrook became another guy who affected me in a major way. Once again, encouragement.

All those guys from that show were really nice to me. They even brought me back to play the lead guest star, *twice*. We did one episode in a courtroom, and the bailiff was a guy named Alvy Moore, who played Hank Kimball, the county agent on *Green Acres* who used to say, "Well, I'm not exactly the county agent . . ." That guy. So here were all these big famous actors, and I just stood in a corner with the guy from *Green Acres* all day. Most people on the set didn't even know who he was, but I'm like, "That's fucking Hank Kimball from *Green Acres*! Don't you know your ass from your elbow?"

That rolled over into Linda Bloodworth and Harry Thomason asking me if I would like to star in their new show *Hearts Afire* with John Ritter and Markie Post. I accepted, and on the show I got real close with John. I knew he had been on TV, but I never did watch *Three's Company* a lot. I just didn't watch the sitcoms of the late seventies through the eighties. Sitcoms kind of got over for me right after *All in the Family* and *Sanford and Son*.

Anyway, John was known as a sitcom guy—he was a very boy-next-door *type*—but he had a real sick sense of humor. Real funny and real dark. He was the first guy I put into *Sling Blade*.

CHAPTER TWENTY-NINE

Sling Blade

Takin' those curves just laughin' at fate

Got a big destination that just won't wait

—"Four Wheel Blacktop Tragedy"

(Thornton/Andrew)

I WANT YOU TO DO THIS MOVIE I'M WRITING," I SAID TO RITTER. "I think it's pretty good. I want you to play the part of this gay guy from St. Louis who now lives in this little town." He said, "Yeah, okay, whatever you want, I'll do it." He thought it was just some horseshit that I was shooting on the weekend.

I wrote *Sling Blade* by myself, and nobody wanted to do it. Then I got a call from my agent at William Morris, who said, "This guy that runs a little company in New York, the Shooting Gallery, he hates the Hollywood system as bad as you do. I think you guys should talk. You'd like each other."

So this kid, Larry Meistrich, and I sat in this boardroom thing, and he said, "Look, your agent is a cool dude, and he seems to think you got some talent. We don't have any money to pay anybody, but I've seen *One False Move* and I loved it. If you have anything you'd like to do . . ." Larry Meistrich and these other kids were all production assistants in New York, and some of their dads had money, so they put stuff on their credit cards and made a movie for $60,000.

So I said, "Well, there's this one thing," and right there at the boardroom meeting table I did the character from *Sling Blade,* which I used to do onstage for my one-man show.

"I want to do a movie about *this* guy," I said. He said, "I'll do it. I can't pay you any money, but I will pay you 50 percent of the revenue." I said, "All right."

When it came time to shoot, Ritter couldn't look at me—he'd never seen the character, nobody did. I purposely didn't do the character for the people in the movie, Dwight Yoakam included. So the first time Ritter saw me do the character was actually *in* the movie, and the first scene I shot with him was the one where we're in the café sitting across the table from each other and he tells me he's gay. After he sat down, I went in there, sat down, and started doing that character. Ritter just busted up. He said, "You can't do that." I said, "But this is the character." He said, "You can't make that face, I'm going to laugh every minute." I said, "John, I'm not making a face, that's the guy." And he goes, "You're going to be like that the whole movie?" And I go, "Yeah." He goes, "I can't do this. I can't do this sitting across from you knowing that it's you. I can't do this." I said, "Look, you'll get used to it, don't worry about it." He finally got over it, but the first day was hard because he couldn't keep a straight face.

We made *Sling Blade* for $980,000 and sold it to Harvey and Bob Weinstein over at Miramax for $10 million. I think it was the most money ever paid for an independent film at that point. The Weinsteins know what's good, and they pushed a lot of good movies through that wouldn't have otherwise been seen by the broader public, like *Sling Blade*. I think Dwight knew *Sling Blade* was something different. I don't think Ritter knew what it was.

DWIGHT YOAKAM ON *SLING BLADE*

Have I ever seen Billy Bob Thornton eat? Non-intravenously? I'm trying to remember. Maybe. Once. No, he spit that out, actually.

When I first got the *Sling Blade* script from Billy, I said, laughing at the outrageous reality of it, "My feeling is on Doyle, that character, he's the most frightened guy in the room. As with most bullies, they're bullying because the best defense is an offense." That's kind of how it was written. If you look at the character Doyle's fear points, when he's first introduced to everybody, he's afraid of this guy that's "retarded." "What kind of retard is this? Is this retard going to make me sick?" It was completely based out of reality. The entire screenplay had such an absence of cliché that it was profoundly undeniable as an important kind of cultural observation in film. At the time we were making it, it was left to its own devices. Nobody knew we were making it, nobody cared that we were making it, nobody knew Billy Bob at that time. He hadn't blown up as an artist. He had acted a number of years on TV, but the public and the industry didn't know him and didn't know he was capable of doing what we were doing down there in Arkansas, and I really believe that's why the movie was so effective. It maintained self-irony without descending into petty self-awareness. Colloquial dramas like that can become laughable. The comedic elements that were involved, there were things that were laughably funny in *Sling Blade.* That Doyle character, the first time I read the role, I was on the phone with my then-girlfriend, who lived in New York, and she thought something had happened. I stopped, I couldn't read after a moment because I was liter-ally succumbing to the humor, the absurdity involved in the writing, and the outrageous reality of it. Because it was a guy, not written as an evil guy. It was just one of those guys that Billy knew or I knew that was really tough probably until it came to something that made him about to throw up, wet his drawers, and Doyle also was living in his own fear all the time. He was the most frightened guy in the film. That's what I said to Billy, I said, "Is that the conceit we can approach this with?" and he said, "Yeah." Backing away from the elements of that character, the genius of that movie to me is that it captured Southern culture without succumbing to the kind of grandiose trappings of it. Even Tennessee Williams presented Southern culture in context, but a kind of Gothic portrayal of the South. There's a melodramatic note in Southern culture, but there's, in Billy's interpretation of things, this wonderfully kind of absurdist, banal, flat-line pulse that he captured in that screenplay. As I said, if he could only win one of the two Oscars that he was nominated for, I was thrilled that he got the Oscar for screenplay. I knew he would be nominated again as an actor, and I just thought that it'd be tough to win both. When he won the one, I thought, that's the right one here, if he doesn't win the other one.

I was given the short he did a couple of years earlier, which was an outgrowth of his one-man monologue that he would do onstage as an exercise and as a performance. He would do Karl in the interrogation scene with the journalist, about being released. That was then stretched out into about a twenty-five- or thirty-minute short called *Some Folks Call It a Sling Blade.* Billy reshot all that. That was the opening of the movie, literally up to the part where he gets out of the mental institute. I saw that and went and met him. I said,

"If this has anything to do with what that was, I'm interested."
He said, "I'm finishing the script, the feature-length version,
and I do have a role I think you could pull off because people
have never seen you do this." At that point I think I had done
five films. I don't know if he saw me in *Roswell,* but anyway,
we met and we hung out. It was on the set of *Hearts Afire,*
in the dressing room on the set when he was shooting that
TV series with John Ritter. He said, "I've written something
really great for John Ritter in this," and he explained some
of that character. It was hilarious. And John did an excep-
tional job playing that role. If it had been pushed or shoved
or nudged too far one way or the other, it would not have
resonated as earnestly. So I went home, got the screenplay,
read it, and I knew.

I got the script and read it in January or February. We
didn't get to go shoot until May. I arrived a few days into the
shooting, and Billy said they were holed up doing editing of
dailies in a bank office, some bank building, not in the vault
but they were in an adjacent room in the bank where they
were being loaned space. They didn't have any trailers, they
didn't have any dressing rooms, they strung up sheets, so
he said, "Do you want to watch some of the dailies?" and I
said, "Sure." He played a couple scenes—they had been
shooting four days—and that's when I got on the phone
back to L.A. and told my then–office manager, I said, "I'm
in something pretty real here. This may be something that
really makes a mark, that really has an impact on film viewers." It then took another year and a half to get it done, to
get it sold. He sold it to Miramax in the spring of '96. It was
almost a year later, and they held it until the fall of '96, actually December of '96 it came out. It came out Thanksgiving

week in just small theaters, and it qualified, and then they ran it for the Academy Awards.

It's really tough for Billy to collaborate with film companies. It has been and will be because it's such a seminal, almost singular cultural moment, that film, a statement of culture. It so captured the nuance of Southern American culture, and because it was so absent the kind of grandiose, Gothic, Tennessee Williams–esque proscenium presentation of it all. It transcended Southern culture and really captured American rural and common culture. Working-class culture in America. I've had people from Wisconsin to Washington State to Maine to Texas say, "My brother-in-law is just like that guy." So it resonated, and ironically, it didn't get the kind of huge box office push it might have now or otherwise. It sort of had its longer-lasting impact, I've found, in the ensuing years on television when people would watch it on DVD.

It's a great role. On the page it was brilliantly written. There were only two ad-libs, and he let me do them. One was on the floor after the kid, Lucas Black, ran out of actual prop material to throw, so he started throwing real books and real things, and I got hit a couple times with some real stuff. I was on my knees, and I looked down and the ad-lib was, "Fuck me." He left that. And there were a couple of other moments—the blow-up scene with the band. I think "you tuning son-of-a-bitch" was not on the page. It was such a gracious script for an actor. I think every actor involved would say that. Every character written in there, from the character that Rick Dial—God rest his soul, he recently passed—he played the lawn mower shop owner who told the joke about two guys peeing off the bridge and Karl tried to repeat later.

There was the Scooter role. Billy deftly executes one of the great watercolor cinematic paintings in terms of every nuanced piece of dialogue, the way that Lucas Black's character Frank speaks with Karl. The way Karl speaks with Frank, the way I speak with Frank—"Frankie, the adults are talking." "You're a weird little shit, Frank." All that was just singularly unique in its ability to capture and convey the absurdly banal and often tragic existence of common lives.

I don't think *Sling Blade* aspired to the moralizing heights that *To Kill a Mockingbird* did. *To Kill a Mockingbird,* in a strange way, doesn't have the gravitas of *Sling Blade.* Because it doesn't ever make an attempt to preach or condescend in any moment. *Sling Blade* is like *Hud,* although I think *Sling Blade* had a greater cultural access point than *Hud.* There's a duality to him and to life, Hud, Doyle, in this, that you actually, while not approving of him, you can't help but like him. "I don't approve of you at all, Hud, but I like you and I feel sorry for you." There's a sorrow to that guy Hud. There's a sad tragedy to that guy. I believe it's true what they say about directing—that 90 percent of great directing is casting properly. I believe that with everything. I don't know what Billy feels, but I would think he would think that you can only do so much if it's the wrong person cast.

We weren't friends before *Sling Blade.* He didn't know me. I'd never met him. First of all, I said, "Somebody's yanking your chain." I said that to Darris Hatch, my then-theatrical manager who had been my agent for a year. She said, "You've got to set that meeting up, for Billy Bob," and I'm like, "Hold it. This is someone yanking my chain. Ain't nobody named Billy Bob in Los Angeles that's writing movies and putting me in them. They're pulling on the cowboy hat wearing hillbilly singer's chain. Boy wants to be in a movie, tell him Billy Bob wants to meet him."

The funniest thing that ever happened with me with Billy Bob was the movie *Don't Look Back,* an HBO film, and he had me cast in it—that was after *Sling Blade*—before it came out. We were acting this scene where he kills my character, who was as nervous as a cat. We're about to play billiards, and he stabs me to death with a cheese knife. So they put blood capsules in my mouth so they could do it. They did a couple of dry takes. They had replaced the first director, and the guy they brought in was this colorful English director. Billy and I were in the middle of this scene, and they had overfilled my mouth with makeup blood. Billy and I were literally inches apart, face-to-face, and this is a guy who is completely, utterly germ-aware. And he said something and did something, and it was a blown take. He had stabbed at me, and I couldn't catch myself and blurted out an entire mouthful of makeup blood. He had it all over his face, all over his chest, it dripped down his face, and I couldn't stop laughing because I knew how horrified he was. It's spilling out of my mouth, saliva and makeup blood that I had been holding in my mouth for about a minute and a half, waiting for this take, and it was literally like somebody had come along with a gun nozzle and sprayed him to the wall. The horror on his face—I was on the floor on my hands and knees trying to cough, to choke from laughing, cough, and saying I was sorry at the same time. I was so sorry, and the more I said it, the more I laughed because I knew how horrified he was by the element of . . . God bless him, I guess he didn't become sick from it, I was germ-free to some extent, but still, the idea of him in that clumsy moment, he had stabbed at me already, and I had jerked away because I was choking because the guy had filled me up with too much blood. It was a series of things that led up to this split-second moment where I literally sprayed him with spit and makeup blood. And the horror of that was the funniest thing I've ever witnessed with Billy Bob Thornton, and the ensuing attempt at apologizing on the floor when I was literally coughing up makeup blood and laughing incessantly. I was like a hyena. The second it happened, it's like a sneeze that goes off and you've got a mouth full of food with a sneeze, it's the equivalent of, "Oh shit, I'm going to sneeze, and I have this mouth full of food, and I can't sneeze and HUYYAHHH!" There's no delicate way for that to come off, and it went face-first into him. He asked me, "What was the funniest thing that you ever saw happen to Billy Bob?" I said, well, I was a party to it. That, to this day, is still the funniest moment. That and the Gary Busey moment that I can't go into. Gary Busey was telling me a very funny story about Strother Martin doing something to him, and in the process of telling it Gary Busey proceeded to goose Billy Bob up his ass and walk him around the room with his hand on his ass. Again, it was a moment if he would have had a hatchet, he would've chopped his way out of it. At the moment there weren't any hatchets available, and he couldn't get away from the storytelling hand of Gary Busey.

CHAPTER THIRTY

John Ritter

WHEN RITTER FIRST GOT THERE, WE WERE STAYING AT THE RAMADA Inn in this little town we were shooting in, Benton, Arkansas. We had a makeup girl and then a hair girl. The hair girl really didn't do hair, she did makeup, but we didn't have a lot of money for anything and she was friends with the girl doing makeup. Her name's Kate, good gal, now she's a huge makeup artist. So I told Kate, "Look, here's what we want for Ritter. I want you to give him a kind of flattop or one of those hairdos that goes up in the air like gay dudes have. Something kind of hip-looking . . . but not *quite*."

Here's the story: Ritter's character is a gay man from St. Louis who works for a chain of Dollar Stores. They transfer him to this little town in Arkansas. We never *said* it was Arkansas, but it was a little state. Anyway, he still gets all the magazines he subscribed to in St. Louis—*GQ* and shit like that—in this little one-horse town. He takes his copy of *GQ* down to the local barber shop, and he shows them a picture and says, "I want to look like that." So it's Peggy from Millsburg's version of this *GQ* haircut.

"I want it dyed," I told Kate, "and I want him to be blond." And Ritter goes, "Well, I got to do something when I get back to L.A." He had to do some public service announcements for something, I can't remember what they were for, but he said, "Don't go too crazy with it."

"Don't worry about it," I said.

So, we're in his motel room at the Ramada Inn, and he's sitting there. There's no mirror in front of us. Kate dyes his hair first. It comes out red and black. It's, like, maroon and black in the movie, but you know hair dye—when you first do it, it takes a couple of hours before it settles in. Then she cuts his hair. She gives him fucking whitewalls on the side and a flattop standing straight up in the air, and I look at Kate and say, "This is perfect. This is fucking genius. I had no idea it was going to be this perfect." Ritter, all excited, goes, "What? What is it? Let me see!"

Ritter goes and looks in the mirror. "I'm going to fucking kill you!" he says. "I look like an idiot! Do you understand that I have to fucking be on television when I get back?!"

"No, this is perfect, it's ideal! This is going to be great! You're going to love it." After the movie was over, he appeared on the PSA for whatever it was with a Dodgers cap.

RITTER WAS ONE OF THE GREATEST FUCKING GUYS. YOU TALK ABOUT A shock when he died.

We had just played Farm Aid in Columbus, Ohio, that past weekend, and I got the flu real bad. I was sick as shit. Columbus was our last date, but I was so sick I couldn't come home after the show. I had to stay in the hotel room there for two or three more days by myself. Everybody else left. (Thanks, guys.) When I got off the stage after the show, Stephen Bruton was there with me, as was Jim Marshall, the photographer. Marshall took pictures of me with Bruton and Dennis Kucinich, the guy that ran for president—he was Willie Nelson's candidate because he was all for pot—standing between the buses and stuff.

Anyway, I was getting sick already and my lungs were on fire. Warren Zevon was my buddy, and he was *real* sick at that time with lung cancer—that mesothelioma or whatever it was he had. After Marshall took these pictures, I did an interview, and they told me Warren had just died. I think that was on Sunday.

I get over this flu enough to fly home. A couple of nights later, I get this call from Jerry, my business manager—who was also Ritter's manager—at midnight. He was all emotional. "We've lost John," he said. "We've lost John." It didn't make any sense to me. I was thinking of my brother because my brother's name is John, so I said, "What do you mean *lost* him? Where the fuck is he?" And he, knowing I didn't understand, goes, "No, John *Ritter*. We lost him." And I'm still not understanding, because when somebody tells me "we lost" somebody, it means they're in Bakersfield and won't tell anybody. "John died," he says.

Dwight called me literally thirty seconds into the conversation with Jerry. Dwight was just calling to bullshit—we talk late at night all the time—and I said, "Dwight, hang on a second, Ritter just died, I'll call you right back."

I got off the phone with Jerry and got back on with Dwight. We talked for three hours about Ritter. But then I woke up the next morning, Johnny Cash had died. The very next morning. Warren Zevon, John Ritter, and Johnny Cash within, like, five days. I was friends with all those guys. Particularly Warren and John, but I knew Cash very well. It was just a strange week.

CHAPTER THIRTY-ONE

You People

There's a life not built for your convenience
And things that happen naturally
That we call experience

—"Look Up" (Thornton/Andrew)

WHEN I FIRST GOT NOMINATED FOR AN ACADEMY AWARD, THE FIRST two people who called me were Elizabeth Taylor and Gregory Peck. I couldn't believe it, could not believe it.

Though I hadn't been famous long, my birthday appeared on the news, on the bottom of the crawl, and I got this voice mail:

"I just wanted to call and say happy birthday, hoss. Waylon Jennings. Give me a call back. I love your movies. That *Sling Blade*, that's something else, man. You hit a home run there, son. Give me a call, hoss, happy birthday."

That was on my voice mail. I called him back, and that's how I got to know Waylon. I loved Waylon. Out of all four of those guys, Willie, Waylon, Cash, and Kris Kristofferson, Waylon was the one I could talk to the easiest. I was always nervous around Cash. I always feel dumb around Kris.

RIGHT AFTER WE'D MADE SLING BLADE, I MET A VERY FAMOUS MOVIE actress and singer at a party with a lot of big stars. That was when I was first getting around big Hollywood people. She was telling me how much she loved *Sling Blade*—such an interesting world, she said, a world she knew nothing about. She said the movie was beautiful and went on and on about it. But then she said, "So where are you from again?" And I said, "Arkansas." And she said, "What do you people do down there?" She actually said, "What do *you* people do down there?"

After years and years of living in California and becoming more sophisticated myself, I'd kind of gotten over a lot of my insecurities and low self-opinion about feeling that I'm some hillbilly who has no business being out here. I mean, I went from being this three-year-old kid running around with a fucking World War I gas mask on, getting his ass beat with a razor strap, pissing in the yard, watching knife fights with my uncle, living among people who nail their wives up in the house and make their kids eat mustard and biscuits, to a guy standing in a major party in Malibu with all these big stars—I remember Mel Gibson was there, and Lionel Richie was playing piano—and there I was, being asked by this very rich, enormously famous singer-actress person, "What do *you* people do down there?"

After that night I told somebody the story, and they said she was raised kind of normally—she wasn't like some rich sophisticate—so it was more like the regional thing than it was the money thing. She just didn't know that world I came from, but to actually have somebody say that to me—it made me think about the different ethnic groups who have had that said to them before. "*You* people." I'll never forget it because it made me feel like, "Oh yeah. I forgot. I'm still just a hillbilly from Arkansas."

Anyway, I remember afterward going outside and having a smoke by myself on this big veranda. The house was out by a hill and the ocean, and I was kind of just walking around, looking out at Malibu, thinking, *Goddamn.* You know? *It still shows, don't it?*

I've never gotten over it. Not her comment—I'm not that fucking thin-skinned—but I've never gotten over my belief that I'm not as good as most people. I still have a real low opinion of myself. As I said, my belief in myself—which has gotten me to this point—has a lot to do with ignorance. Sometimes I just don't know any better. People used to ask, "When you came to California, if it was so fucking hard all those years, why didn't you go back?" I'd say, "What would I go back to?" It wasn't like it was any better for me back there. I was broke as shit when I came to California. But if I had known how long it was going to take . . . I don't know, I always thought tomorrow was the day. I've thought that since I was a little kid. I always thought that tomorrow everything's going to be all right. I'm still kind of like that. I'm the most pessimistic optimist you'll ever meet.

CHAPTER THIRTY-TWO

Viva la Independence

THE REASON SOME PEOPLE CAN'T ARTICULATE WHY THEY LIKE INDE-pendent films as opposed to commercial films is that in the independent film it's about the *people* who are involved in it, not just Handsome Actor X. If you watch these standard $100 million action movies, more often than not Handsome Actor X is there to kill all the bad guys and ends up doing the thing he's set out to do, get out of the pickle he's in, save whatever it is he's supposed to save, get the dope, get the money, or whatever it is. The bad guys are nameless, faceless characters who you know goddamn well are just going to get killed by Handsome Actor X. It's not important who they are or where they came from, so as a result you're not afraid of the bad guy, and the feeling you get from the commercial movie is not profound.

But if you see a mobster in a movie sitting down to dinner with his family, playing with his son, giving him a toy—a little rabbit or some shit—talking to his wife about how the power's out in the garage, all of a sudden you got a real guy. If you got three scenes of a real guy playing with his kids, fixing the garage door opener, watching Lucy and Desi on TV, and laughing at it because Lucy got into another mess and Ricky ain't going to let her sing, and then getting in his Cadillac to drive across town where he goes to a building and waits around the corner for a woman in a red dress who comes walking out and he comes up behind her and puts a .22 caliber hollow-point in the back of her head, then fixes his briefcase and gets back into his car, you're scared of that motherfucker—all because he gave the kid the rabbit. If you never saw him give the kid the rabbit, you're not afraid of him because *he ain't real.*

There are things that they market the shit out of that make a lot of money. There are things that aren't marketed that sometimes do well and sometimes don't. We rely on critics and awards for these kinds of movies to take off because they're not going to put big money toward marketing them. But you can't really *rely* on marketing anyway. When I did *Sling Blade,* I thought the critics would love it, but I thought maybe my mom, a few family members, and friends would see it. I thought it was going to be one of those little movies that a handful of people saw and liked. It turned out to be hugely successful. Because then critics weren't snot-sucking guys on the Internet and it got good word of mouth.

I've got a couple of things so far that have become iconic in some way, and that's been a great thing. Especially since I'm alive to see it. But I was lucky that I became a legitimate movie star. Most people become movie stars because of the way they look—they're twenty-three and look like models—but I became a movie star by playing extreme characters from the beginning, which allowed me a lot of freedom. It gave me longevity, because while an audience might accept me as a leading man, I can go back and play an extreme character again because that's the way audiences first came to know me. They'll buy me doing a guy in *Monster's Ball* and *The Man Who Wasn't There,* but they'll also buy me as a character actor in *A Simple Plan* or *Sling Blade.*

I think everybody has at some point done movies for money.

When you watch an actor do a movie that's obviously not their bag, you'll see them use the same tricks in that movie as they did in that other movie they did for money because their heart and soul aren't in it.

I honestly feel bad for the top leading actors who want to explore other characters and do independent films when the audience only wants to see them be the handsome hero. The audience just won't buy them doing other stuff.

But the reason actors want to do independent films is that an independent film—and this is the artistic part of it—is usually more narrowed down to a singular vision. It's more pure, and it's going to tell the best story. And when you're doing an independent film, you can cast the best actors for parts. In a commercial film, because of the money they're spending, they want the guy who was just in that $500 million movie. The movie that you're making for $4 million, they don't give a shit as much, though even that is changing.

INDEPENDENT FILM HAS CHANGED IN THE LAST TEN OR TWELVE YEARS. When I started out in it, it was *completely* pure. It got soiled when actors saw they were making these great films that used to be called "B movies," and all of a sudden they're called "independent" and have a cachet. The studios say, "Well, we can't pay you." And the actor says, "That's okay, I'll do it for nothing because I want to be in a good film. The last movie I was in, I was playing a dog that turns into a Martian, and I don't want to do that shit anymore."

So they're now going to do an independent film because they want to use their acting chops and be in a great film that tells a real story. Then the independent film studios say, "Look, we don't have to go get the big actor for $10 million anymore. We can make a $3 million movie, and because he or she wants to make a good movie, they'll come do it for nothing." All of a sudden, instead of the $5 million independent film having a bunch of unknowns and maybe a couple of guys you've heard of before, even the hatcheck girl is being played by a big movie star. I'm not saying independent film is completely ruined. I'm just saying it's gone down the wrong path. If you're going to make the independent film the same way you make the commercial movie, then what's the point?

MY BEST ADVICE FOR A YOUNG FILMMAKER OR ACTOR, MUSICIAN, OR writer who doesn't give a shit—the guy who just wants to go out there and make a movie with a bunch of toys and shit like that—is to spend your life doing the physics of it. Find out what button it is that you push out here that makes you a star.

I've always admired William Goldman, who wrote *Butch Cassidy and the Sundance Kid, A Bridge Too Far,* and many other movies. He wrote a book called *Adventures in the Screen Trade,* so if you want to be a screenwriter, read that book. He'll tell you what it's like dealing with people. It was something that was invaluable to me and to Tom Epperson when we were coming up. It's kind of the bible for screenwriters in a lot of ways. The book doesn't tell you how to write a screenplay, it tells you what it's like once you *do* start going down that path.

Right now, they're making 3-D vampire movies, or they're making CGI movies where they give a guy a six-pack abdomen with a computer. They're making movies that are basically from video games and directing them at fourteen-year-olds. Well, if that's what you want, if you could give a shit about art, and if all you want is to make a movie that's going to make a gajillion dollars and make you the biggest director of horseshit in the world, then sit down and figure out the science of it. Go see the worst fucking shit you've ever seen in your life—watch *all* the horseshit that's out there—and copy down that formula. It won't take you long. Just know that whereas a commercial film is trying to appeal to a broad audience, an independent film usually does not appeal to the lowest common denominator.

But I would tell young filmmakers who *love* movies that independent film is still the best way to break in. That's where you'll do your best work. People may not like it, they may like it and not like you in it, but one way or the other, it's honest. That's why people do independent film, because you can be honest. Even though I said these days they've been ruined some because they're becoming commercialized, independent film still allows you to start out as an expert in what you're doing—to direct or write or act in the vein you grew up in. As I said, your best work is going to be what you know. If you're a writer, just sit down and write a short story about something that happened to you when you were twelve, I don't care what it is. Like, if you're a guy who grew up on a farm in Georgia, write about a farm in Georgia. You'll be an expert in that.

The Coen brothers, until recently, haven't really done their movies in a studio system. Their movies are generally financed outside the box by people who *get* them, and they've had financial successes doing movies that became bigger movies than what the concept might've been. In other words, the Coen brothers don't set out to make a big commercial movie, though now they have with *True Grit* and the Cormac McCarthy thing. They did set about to make bigger movies there.

CHAPTER THIRTY-THREE

Black and White

THE COEN BROTHERS ARE SOME OF THE GREATEST PEOPLE TO WORK with, they're amazing. They know just what they want. I do quite a bit of improvisational acting in movies, but the couple of times I've been in a Coen brothers movie I did pretty much what they said. I improvised a little bit in *Intolerable Cruelty.* In that movie, they told me to throw out a couple of things that I wanted to do, but their stuff is so tightly written that you don't have to ad-lib. You don't find the need to.

The Man Who Wasn't There, which was set in 1949 and filmed in black and white, was beautifully shot by Roger Deakins and beautifully edited, written, and directed by Joel and Ethan. The film has that whole film noir thing. During the filming of *The Man Who Wasn't There,* I had the flu for the last two weeks, and if you ever see the movie again, in some of the barbershop scenes, which were shot toward the end, you'll notice that I'm a little stuffed up and my eyes are puffy. But that was one of my favorite movies that I've ever been in. Angie always loved that character Ed Crane.

It was largely ignored in the United States because it *is* in black and white, and a lot of people won't watch black-and-white movies. I think black and white is heavier than color. It gives the film a heavier mood. If you watch the old black-and-white movies, they have a different feeling about them, and I wish they made more of them. To me, black and white seems more like reality than a color movie, even though real life is in color. Somehow, black and white makes me feel like I'm in the story more. It's just got something. It's sweaty, it's got depth and character. Think about all the great black-and-white photographs over the years. Usually you don't see those famous photographs of people in color. They're usually black and white, and there's a reason for that.

I've seen pictures from the set of *The Man Who Wasn't There* in color before, and it always upsets me because I just want to think of it in black and white. And there was a great cast of characters, terrific actors. The Coen brothers have a bunch of actors they like to use in their movies, and they know who's right for the parts. I loved working with Fran McDormand and James Gandolfini, but all the actors in the movie were outstanding.

CHAPTER THIRTY-FOUR

A Singular Vision

NOW, I'M NOT ONE WHO SHITS ON COMMERCIAL FILMS BECAUSE they're commercial. I mean, some of them are good. Once again, it's not about how much money is spent, or whether it's independent or commercial. It's, is it good or not? You could say that *Butch Cassidy and the Sundance Kid* is a commercial film, but it happened to be a *good* commercial film. I think *Witness* was a good commercial film. I think *Rocky* was a good commercial film. That was Stallone's vision. No one knew who he was.

Once art becomes anything other than a singular vision—and I'm not saying it has to be *one* guy or *one* girl, it can be a trio of people or whatever, I'm sure you've collaborated with people before—but one way or the other, art has to come from people who are headed toward the same goal.

When they started testing everything—okay, look, you can test a tube of toothpaste and have people taste it and go, "Yeah, it's a little gritty, and it's not quite as sweet as this other one." Okay, fine, do that. You got to put the stuff in your mouth. But art by nature is a vision, a singular *vision*.

Let's take Edward Hopper, he's one of my favorites. Edward Hopper is doing a painting. Let's suppose that in that painting you have a director, a producer, and a studio just as you do in movies. In this scenario, Hopper is the writer and actor, and he shows his painting to Bud and Carl, the producer and the director. They say, "Yeaahhhh, Edward, it's nice, real nice, I like that, it's kinda moody. We're just afraid that it's kinda lonely for what we're going for here."

And Edward Hopper responds, "Well, that's the point. The goddamn painting is called *Loneliness*. It's a woman sitting on the edge of her bed in a seedy motel with a motel sign outside and a diner on the corner. And you're supposed—"

"Yeah, yeah," the producer interrupts, "we get that, but the problem with it is, we don't really know what she's thinking. We want the people who come to our art shows to know what the painting means. We want them to know what she's thinking. So let's just say she's not sitting on the bed, just motionless like that, staring at the wall. What if she's looking out the window at that diner? Then we think maybe she's waiting on someone to show up at that diner."

Hopper says, "Well, the point of this is, we don't know what she's thinkin'."

"Why would you want a painting where nobody knows . . ." and a big argument erupts.

Hopper storms out of the room saying, "Fuck you guys." But those guys put up the money, so the next thing you know there is no Edward Hopper. His name's on it, but the producer's and director's names are on it too. Now the painting is a lot brighter, the colors aren't muted like other Edward Hopper paintings. It's red and blue and the diner's brighter. She's looking out the window with the suggestion of a smile on her face, so you know she's probably waiting on some dude who's coming to the diner, who she's in love with. *Now* you got a painting!

It shouldn't be that way. And that's what I've been dealing

with ever since I tried to be any kind of an artist. I use Edward Hopper's paintings as inspiration for my production design when we make movies. *Sling Blade* was made based on the look of an Edward Hopper painting and the feel of an Edward Hopper painting. That's what I always try to do.

But the fact of the matter is, Edward Hopper didn't have to go to Denver, Seattle, Minneapolis, and Dallas and have a bunch of people in stretch pants say they didn't like his painting, or tell Picasso the eyes were off-center. "Why are the eyes not together? We think you ought to put the eyes on the same level like real people's eyes are." The next thing you know, there wouldn't have been a Picasso. Unfortunately, we work in a business where they can actually tell you how they want you to end a movie. Art no longer exists when the audience is the judge before it's finished, or before it's put out to the public. How is it art? It can't be. They've already screwed it up. If the people can create what they want to see, who cares? I'm not saying that you're supposed to like everything, I'm saying you should have the opportunity to like or dislike something based on a single vision because if it's not that, it's not art. There's bad art, good art, mediocre art, kind of good art, all kinds. That's the beauty of it. If the audience has already become the artist, then it's not art.

When I finished *Sling Blade* and sold it to the distributors, they wanted me to cut the movie down to under two hours. Now, I'd already made a deal with the people who financed it that I had final cut, so the distributors couldn't do anything about it, but I called Martin Scorsese to ask his opinion.

Scorsese is the kind of guy who really studies films. He grew up as a rabid fan of filmmaking—the technical part of it as well as the artistic part of it—and he'll sit down and talk about movies, he knows them all. Scorsese happened to be a fan of *One*

False Move, which was a critical success as an independent film but didn't make me a household name. He said, "If you ever need anything, call me," so I called him.

First, I talked to the lady who ran his company, telling her, "I finished my first theatrical movie as a director and they want me to cut it down. I think it needs to stay the way it is. Am I crazy? Would you look at this? If *you* think I should cut it down, I would do that—I would listen to someone like you—but I just don't want to do it randomly."

She told me to send it, and I did. I didn't hear for two or three weeks, so I just thought he hated it—this was before I knew people didn't call you back for three weeks. But he finally called and said, "Don't cut a frame of this. I happen to think this movie is great the way it is, but I'm not kissing your ass or anything. I'm telling you not to cut this for a whole other reason. Right now, you're under the radar, nobody knows who you are. This is the only time in your career where you're ever going to be able to make a movie *exactly* the way you want it."

This is exactly the opposite of the way I *thought* it worked. I thought you could do anything you want once you get famous, but the truth is, once you get famous, they're gunning for you every minute and you never get to do it your way again.

When you're a famous guy, working with the big boys and making bigger movies, everybody tries to control you. Scorsese was absolutely right. I've never done anything exactly the way I've wanted to do it since.

CHAPTER THIRTY-FIVE

Things Are Fucked Up at the North Pole

WHAT'S GREAT ABOUT *BAD SANTA* IS THAT IT HAD AN INDEPENDENT film feel as well as a commercial movie feel about it. I think the independent feel it had was a tribute to Terry Zwigoff, who is a great independent filmmaker. But just by nature the movie had a commercial appeal. It also had the late, great John Ritter, who did an amazing job, not to mention Brett Kelly—the kid— Lauren Graham, Bernie Mac, Tony Cox, all the other great characters and terrific people.

When Geyer Kosinski, my manager, first sent me the *Bad Santa* script, I thought, *Wow, this is either going to ruin me or it's going to be amazing.* I'd read about a third of it, then I called him and said, "I have to do this movie." I laughed on every page, it was hysterical. It was the most well-reviewed comedy of that year and made a shitload of money. It's been a very successful movie over the years. Every holiday a lot of people include it on their list for watching. I have people say, "Every year we watch *It's a Wonderful Life, Miracle on 34th Street,* and *Bad Santa.*" It's an odd pairing, but I guess some people were tired of the commercialism of Christmas.

There was a lot of carousing going on during that period of time. At the time I was living with my buddy Harve Cook, my video playback guy and one of the producers on this Willie Nelson documentary we did. Harve is a black guy with long dreadlocks from Minneapolis, but his family is from Pine Bluff, Arkansas, and we had a two-year Lost Weekend here at the house. I was single. It was after Angie and I had split up. We'd have thirty, forty, fifty of the cast and crew here on school nights, when we had to be at work at seven in the morning. It was probably the craziest time I ever had. It's also when I met Connie. Her sister Carrie was the makeup artist on the movie, and Connie came to visit her. A couple years later, Connie got pregnant with Bella, so funny enough, I always think how Bella really came about because of my meeting Connie on the set of *Bad Santa*. Today Connie, Bella, and Willie and Harry, my sons, are the center of my universe.

But the truth is, comedy sets are not always fun, happy places. *Bad Santa* was actually kind of a dark set a lot of the time, but I think a lot of the humor actually *came* out of that. I loved playing the character, and we're talking about doing a sequel. People say, "Ah, sequels are always bad," but they're not *always*. It depends on how you approach a sequel. The best thing about *Bad Santa* is it was a movie that didn't follow any rules. Certain people said that we'd ruined the name of Jesus and Santa Claus. Well, first of all, I've read the Bible, and I promise you that it doesn't mention Santa Claus *anywhere,* so you're getting your stories mixed up. Santa Claus has nothing to do with Jesus other than for some reason they made some arbitrary birthday for Jesus and tied Santa Claus into it. Second thing is, *Bad Santa* is not about Santa Claus or Jesus. I play a thief who dresses up like Santa Claus in order to get jewels and shit. If I dressed up like Richard Nixon, would they have been offended? I don't understand it. A thief will dress up like whatever he's got to dress up like. I like *Bad Santa* not just because it's irreverent, but because, in darkly comedic fashion, we both made a statement about the commercialism of Christmas and showed that even the lowest shit on earth can actually have a heart when he sees himself in a kid. It's like, "Wow, I was one of those things one time, wasn't I?"

We want to do a sequel because it's a holiday movie, I enjoyed doing the first one, and people found it to be a good alternative to a corny Christmas movie. Why not do it again? Like I said, I'm not against movies for entertainment's sake—not every movie needs to be earth-shattering. I was a big fan of *The Ghost and Mr. Chicken* with Don Knotts, so clearly I don't mind being entertained. My point is that even if you're going to make entertainment films, make good ones. You can make a $100 million movie that's good and you can make a $1 million movie that's good. *Bad Santa* was successful, so as long as we're all inspired, why not get the team back together to do it again?

Plus, people like to see me play a cynical fuck. I've had eight-year-olds come up to me and say, "Bad Santa!" and I'm like, "God, you let your kid watch that?"

ROBERT DUVALL ON BILLY BOB THORNTON

I asked my wife the other night to give me her commentary on Billy Bob. She reflected for just a brief moment and then said with quiet conviction that he is very intuitive with actors when he deals with them and he does so in a very offhand way, obviously with great understanding. I find my wife to be extremely smart about such things. What she said struck a corresponding conclusion within me.

Although he is quite disciplined in his framing of scenes, he still—as I saw it—works in flashes, extremely personal flashes. Other directors work this way I'm sure, but I haven't always been aware. His flashes are unique to him and right on the money.

We are all one of a kind, but Billy seems to be one of a kind and more.

The common denominator of truth is pretty much in evidence in his work—throughout!

He asks for no rehearsals. He says rehearsals are for "pussies." If he then goes beyond two takes, it is indeed unusual. So in a sense he ends up shooting the rehearsal anyway.

He tries to stay away from preconceptions as much as possible. I feel it's better to come in and start from zero and then see where it goes from there. I think Billy would agree with this.

As a fine actor himself, I'm sure he ducks when he sees the milkman coming. So many directors will milk the crap out of a scene until there is nothing left. They continue to overlook what they are looking for, and after forty or fifty takes, it's a bit of a joke! Boys like Kubrick made outstanding movies but often had one or two performances that pretty much sucked! Too many takes.

Not so with directors like Coppola, Altman, or Billy Bob.

Actors will say, what is it like to work with this director or that one? The one conclusion that keeps being repeated is that the preferred directors are the ones that "leave you alone."

When decent, intelligent direction is given, you listen. He gave me a brilliant piece of direction toward the end of *Jayne Mansfield's Car.* It came out of nowhere, but it was spot-on!

Billy's set at times is like adult day camp. Fun and games in and around the set is his approach. One time he stopped shooting and said something to the effect of, "Come on, guys, we're getting too serious here. Filming should be fun, and we are here to do that." He seems extremely relaxed as a director even in the most serious situations, and believe me, that attitude permeates the entire set!

Billy is a triple threat—writing, acting, directing—I don't know what kind of training he ever had, nor do I care. He has a deep cultural understanding of who he is and what he comes from—language!—and he understands the journey from ink to behavior about as good as anybody.

Maybe he just looked in the mirror one day and said, "Hey, Billy, let's just go and do it." Let's get out of here before the milkman comes!!!

CHAPTER THIRTY-SIX

On the Front Porch: Conversations with Daniel Lanois

Part 1

DANIEL LANOIS: I always felt that *All the Pretty Horses* was a daunting task because of the thickness of the book. How do you go about taking such a complex adventure and try and rein that into a digestible cinematic experience, without having an intermission?

BILLY BOB THORNTON: If I had had my way and if you had had your way, it probably *would* have had an intermission. The original cut of that movie was the one with your score in it and that is the thing I felt we made. *That's* the movie we made that I was proudest of. Matt Damon, to this day, still calls it a masterpiece. The people who saw that original cut with your score in it have said the same thing.

I wasn't the one who had to rein it in. Ted Tally wrote the script and that's something I'm not good at. I'm not good at adapting other people's stuff. I never was. I got my bag that I kind of do, and I feel I can do what *I* do pretty well, but I could never take someone else's book and write a screenplay based on it. This sounds really shitty maybe but I don't know that I'd be interested enough to. I have too much stuff I want to say, myself. So I don't know that I would ever choose to be someone who adapts. Which is ironic because I have an Academy Award for Best Screenplay, based on other material—but it was my own material. It was based on the short film that I wrote as well as the stage stuff I did with that character.

I don't think I could have reeled in *All the Pretty Horses*. Directing it was a different thing because I had the script already and I had a clear vision of how to direct *that* script, but it was Ted Tally's script so the credit all goes to him in terms of how you pare that book down into a movie. It was still a daunting task to direct something that big.

I was told, and we may as well talk about it because we've never done that other than amongst each other, at night, with a bottle of whiskey—I was told by the studio people, without mentioning any names, that a producer had watched the movie with his wife and his wife felt that the music was too sparse. I had a screaming argument with him on the phone. He said that we were going to have a different score. I said, "Honestly"—and I'm not just saying this, I've said it to everybody ever since— "that was *the* best and the most haunting musical score for a movie I've ever heard in my lifetime. Ever." And to this day it is. That's why I'll beg you someday because that would be a great thing for us to put in a movie, that score on some movie, and we'll find the right one where we can make it and the lawyers won't fuck it up.

Just like taking that score out of the movie, the cut was the same thing. And the big news in the papers, when I had the big argument with the studio, was that I had some four-hour cut that I wanted to put out and that was never the truth. My final cut was two hours and forty-two minutes, which is the exact length of the *English Patient,* made by the one of the studios that made *All the Pretty Horses.*

They told me in the beginning that they knew this was an epic movie and it would be a three-hour movie—they told me that up front—and then proceeded to cut it to under two hours (an hour and fifty-nine minutes), and that was just an arbitrary cut to get it down to under two hours because they get more showings in the theaters. It wasn't done for creative reasons; it was done for length reasons. It was marketed as a love story between Matt and Penélope and that's not what the story was. If there was a love story there, it was between the two kids, Henry and Matt. The movie was about the end of the west as we know it. It wasn't a love story between a guy and a girl, but at the time *Titanic* was popular and I begged the studio, "Please don't make the poster where Matt and Penélope are all airbrushed and staring at each other like the *Titanic* poster," and sure enough, that's what they put out.

Every step along the way they took the soul out of what it was and that's why the movie did not do well, because you can't put something out half-assed. If you put it out as a romantic story like *Titanic,* which is not what it is, then that audience goes to see it and they don't like it because they thought they were going to see a love story between the pretty guy and girl. The audience who wants to see a Cormac McCarthy book on film, they don't get the whole story and then they're disappointed. That's why when you make something, you have to put it out the way it was intended. It has to be what it is. If you try to take an apple into an orange, you're going to lose both sides of the audience— the commercial audience you're trying to sell it to and the real audience that wants to see it. That's what happened with *All the Pretty Horses*. We made a beautiful thing and I'll love it forever, and people ask me still to this day, why don't you guys put out your real cut of it?

DANIEL LANOIS: Do you have it? Do you have the film with my score on it?

BILLY BOB THORNTON: I have it in the house; I've actually shown it to people before. I have it on VHS tape. I've got every tape— I've got the dailies, I've got every tape all along the way of all the footage, *with* the score in it, and I've got the complete movie with the score. I actually have the whole assembly with your score. The three hours and something. I've got that, too.

Years ago, when they talked to me about doing the DVD, at one point the studio actually called me and said they'd give me the opportunity to put your cut out on DVD, but I turned it down because this was back when we were still feeling pretty raw from it. We were feeling a little beat-up and you weren't real keen on giving them your score to put on the DVD when they didn't put it in the fucking movie on the big screen. I agreed with you, and said no, I stand with my pal Dan. I won't do it unless his score is in it. That's why I never did it. It deserved to be seen and it deserved to have that music, but I have to say, we gave the actors some of the music during the making of the movie and they listened to it as inspiration for their characters. They'll tell you, any one of them, to this day, that it's the most haunting music they've ever heard.

DANIEL LANOIS: I remember I bumped into Penélope Cruz in France at Cannes. I didn't know her. I had just met her briefly with you, and she came up to me and she said, "Are you Daniel Lanois?" I said, "Yes." She said, "That was the most beautiful music that you made for the film and I'm so sorry it didn't come out."

BILLY BOB THORNTON: They all felt that way; every one of them felt that way.

DANIEL LANOIS: To not use that piece of music for the train station scene, that's a crime.

BILLY BOB THORNTON: That *is* a crime. And the whole process of how it was done, not only the Teatro, but coming down there with Emmylou (Harris) at that big old building down there in Texas and her singing there for the crew and recording it and you guys being the band on the stage—the way everything was going about, it was a great story and a great experience making that movie. We made a classic, and nobody is ever going to see it.

I've told a couple of critics before that maybe someday I would show it to them. I told Robert Ebert that I was going to show it to him. I'd like to. I have it all on VHS tape sitting up there at the house. For me, I only played it for a couple of people because I wanted these particular people to see it, but it was hard for me to watch it knowing that, you know—it's heartbreaking to watch the beauty of what we did at that time. The movie came out, it was a good movie, but it wasn't what we made. That ranks as my biggest disappointment.

DANIEL LANOIS: I know you put a lot of work into it.

BILLY BOB THORNTON: You did too. It was a pretty amazing experience. I still think of some of those guys that played on there that we hung out with at that time, like Vic. Remember Vic, the drummer?

DANIEL LANOIS: Yeah. Great drummer. To this day, great.

BILLY BOB THORNTON: And Russ the Bus.

DANIEL LANOIS: Fish out some of that music sometimes. There's one track called, uh, . . . I played it for Keisha [Kalfin] a couple of weeks ago . . . called Steppin' Wolf [hums].

BILLY BOB THORNTON: Oh yeah, it was fantastic. That was Vic.

DANIEL LANOIS: That was Vic playing that corrugated kind of agüero-like stick.

BILLY BOB THORNTON: Well, there was all that stuff that you did specifically . . . some of the pieces were things you had around for a while, which we kind of based the original vibe on, and then you started doing the stuff that had the real Spanish flavor, Mexican flavor. The song Raul Malo sang, and then . . . did we end up using the Red River Valley theme in that? Because it was a great theme. I don't know if we ever did or not, but it was brought up several times. You went through this whole period where you specifically wrote new things. I have a CD of that stuff, which was quite spectacular. I mean, a lot of it didn't even make *our* cut of it, because there was just a lot of it. I've *got* a lot of it. It's gathered together so you wouldn't have to look for it. I could just give you a CD of your own stuff that's right there together. I've got *all* of that music in the drawer at the house.

CHAPTER THIRTY-SEVEN

A Simple Plan

THERE WERE TWO CHARACTERS THAT I'VE PLAYED WHO I NEVER wanted to stop playing—where when the movie was over I wanted to stay in that character. One was the character in *The Man Who Wasn't There,* the other was my character in *A Simple Plan.* If you put the character from *A Simple Plan* and the character from *The Man Who Wasn't There* together, it's pretty much who I am in real life.

In *A Simple Plan,* I got to be with my old buddy Bill Paxton, who I came up with out here in California; Bridget Fonda, who's terrific; and Brent Briscoe, who I introduced to the film's director, Sam Raimi. "You ought to look at my buddy Brent," I said. "He had a part in *Sling Blade,* and I've known him from the days when we worked on *Evening Shade.*" Brent Briscoe from Moberly, Missouri.

A Simple Plan was filmed up in Ashland, Wisconsin, and Delano, Minnesota. The cast and crew stayed at a haunted hotel in Wisconsin, and it was very, very cold. The wind-chill factor one night was sixty below zero, and Paxton and I were looking at each other, we were shooting outside, and I said, "Bill, what are we going to do? The sound cart is even frozen up. Can we stay out here all night without dying?"

Paxton says, "Dude, I don't know, I'm not sure." But we got through it.

We loved playing those characters. I loved playing Jacob so much, I went a little too far losing weight for the role and later ended up kind of sick and in the hospital. But Sam Raimi directed a beautiful movie, and I got nominated for an Oscar for best supporting actor. Still, I thought that movie didn't get its due like it should have.

ON THE FRONT PORTCH: CONVERSATIONS WITH DANIEL LANOIS

Part II

DANIEL LANOIS: I was quite taken by *A Simple Plan*. Just the most regular people can suddenly get caught up in this fever. Can you tell us a little bit about that?

BILLY BOB THORNTON: *A Simple Plan* was based on a book, and the book was brilliant. The great thing about that movie is that they hired Scott Smith, who wrote the book, to write the script. I think they should do that more often instead of hiring whoever the screenwriter of the day is, because if you have a book that's five hundred or six hundred pages long and you're asked to pare that down to a hundred-and-ten-page movie screenplay, the writer of that book is going to know better than anybody how to do that, how to edit that book. I'd say give a novelist the first crack at making his book into a movie; Scott Smith did and he wrote a brilliant script. The director on that movie—there had been a few—they tried to make that movie several times and it never came together. Different people were attached to it over the years. When I was asked, when they finally got it on its feet and were actually going to make it over at Paramount, John Boorman was the director. John is a classic British director; he directed *Deliverance, Emerald Forest, Hope and Glory, Excalibur*—he's a terrific director and one of my favorites, and a guy that I'd always wanted to work with. I was thrilled and I went out to meet him at the Beverly Wilshire Hotel to talk about being in the movie. He said, "I want to ask you, I really want you to do this movie." He said, "There's just one thing I want to run by you. You may not like this but I'm hoping you will because I'm telling you, I know in my heart this is the way to do it." They were set to shoot in Minnesota. They were already looking into locations because they needed snow.

I said, "Well, before you ask me, can I guess?" And he said, "Sure, go ahead." I said, "You don't want me to play the lead, you want me to play the brother, the second lead, right?" He said, "Exactly." I said, "I was going to ask you if that was okay by you because I want to play that part." And then I suggested Bill Paxton to play the brother and Bill was terrific in it.

As it turns out, though, John Boorman and the studio had some type of falling-out and he didn't do the movie. I was hugely disappointed, but then they got Sam Raimi, who I knew some, and I loved Sam. I thought, *If anybody can pull this off, it's Sam,* so I said I'd love to do it with Sam. We went up there and they didn't have any snow in Minnesota in January/February. The little town that they already scouted didn't have any snow and so we had to move over to a town called Ashland, Wisconsin, up where Michigan and Wisconsin come together on Lake Superior by Canada and, believe me, in January and February there's always some snow.

So here we were, in Wisconsin and Minnesota in January, February, and March. I wanted to be really, really skinny for this movie *Pushing Tin* that we shot in Toronto where you visited me a couple of times. *Pushing Tin* was to start right after *A Simple Plan*. I had already started to get a little bony. I ate one thing every day, the same thing every day, during the making of *A Simple Plan*. I ate a can of tuna and a package of Twizzlers, you know, the red candies?

DANIEL LANOIS: The licorice candy?

BILLY BOB THORNTON: They're like a licorice. I ate that every day for three months and I ended up weighing 135 pounds. I shouldn't have done it. I got a little sick from it. Just like I gained a lot of weight for movies early on—I'll never do that again. That was not fun. It's really hard to lose the weight, and it makes you sick. When I did *Pushing Tin*, I weighed 135 pounds. I think I actually got down to 130 at one point. I was a stick. I only weigh 145 now and people say "hey, you need to put some weight on," but back then it was like ridiculous. What I wasn't thinking was I had started losing the weight for *A Simple Plan* and the character in the book was a huge fat guy. It didn't matter, I played him as that kind of character anyway, but I packed on a lot of clothes for the movie so I didn't look as skinny as I really was. I hadn't thought about how when you're skinny you're just freezing your ass off every minute.

DANIEL LANOIS: You said it got down to sixty below zero. How did you deal with that kind of extreme cold?

BILLY BOB THORNTON: You just have to numb yourself out. After a while you had to get into your character so much you just forgot about it. It was miserable. Sam is a great director. He's a very planned guy. He and the storyboard artist would have dinner together every night and come up with new ways to shoot things so it makes it easier for actors because you always know the camera is going to be in the right place and you can ignore it. Particularly when you're a director yourself, you may want to look over the guy's shoulder and say, "Really, are you sure you want to shoot it that way?" With a guy like Sam Raimi or the Coen brothers, you don't ever think about that.

CHAPTER THIRTY-EIGHT

Pushing Tin

MADE *A SIMPLE PLAN* AND *PUSHING TIN* BACK TO BACK. IN FACT, I only had like a week off in between those movies, so I kind of pair those movies together in terms of that period of my life. *Pushing Tin* is where Angie and I first really got to know each other. It was also the first time I worked with John Cusack, who's just great to work with, and with whom I also later did *The Ice Harvest*. And then, of course, there was the great Cate Blanchett. *Pushing Tin* didn't do great. I think it was three-quarters of a great movie and the last twenty minutes or so, not so much—like some of the critics said, it took off but it didn't land. But I loved the experience and think the part of the movie that *was* good was *terrific*. John and I even went to air traffic control school for the film up there in Toronto, where we filmed. We had to, because you can't spout all that stuff out if you haven't been to school for it. We had a great instructor who was really good to us and took us out on the floor to watch real air traffic controllers. Just so you know, if you're ever going to Newark, New Jersey, and something happens to the controller, I can land the plane.

THE GREATEST THING IS WHEN YOU'RE DOING A MOVIE AND YOU'RE IN a different town, especially a place like Toronto where they're probably making ten movies at one time, and some of your pals are up there too. In this one hotel it was me and the gang from our movie—John Cusack, Cate Blanchett, Angie, and Mike Newell, the director. Ritter was there because he was doing a TV movie with Nicollette Sheridan. Neil Jordan, the British director who did *The Crying Game,* was there. Robbie Robertson was there. Chuck Leavell was there. All the Rolling Stones were there too, because they rehearse up there before they go out on tour. I would go hang out at the bar with Cusack, Ritter, Angie, Nicollette Sheridan, Ronnie Wood, Chuck Leavell, Neil Jordan, and Robbie Robertson. That kind of gang, hanging out at the bar every night, it gets pretty interesting. And then Mick Jagger, who was in the room up above me, he knew I was going through some weird shit in my life at the time, and he would call me up to his room and we'd just sit there and talk about shit for hours. He would drink wine and sometimes play the piano.

This song of mine called "Angelina" that I did on my first album and that we redid for the Boxmasters is about the first day Angie and I got to Toronto. When we were in the elevator.

CHAPTER THIRTY-NINE

Bandits

OUTSIDE OF *JAYNE MANSFIELD'S CAR*, WHICH WE'RE CURRENTLY filming, probably the best experience I've had on a movie in terms of the locations, a cast that got along, and just having a great time was *Bandits*. Barry Levinson was a real entertaining director. He used to keep us rolling. And it was real fun hanging out with Bruce Willis and Cate Blanchett, both of whom were already friends. And the locations were incredible. We started in Portland, Oregon, and worked our way all the way down to L.A., shooting in Salinas, Santa Rosa, Bodega Bay, Half Moon Bay, up in Oregon, Klamath Falls and Oregon City, out at the Columbia River Gorge. Just all these amazing places for the locations. We had the best time on that movie.

At that time I was having a big fight with the studios about *All the Pretty Horses*, and I was under so much stress that my gums were bleeding real bad on set. My makeup artist would have to come up and blot my gums with a tissue between takes. On top of everything else, *Bandits* came out a week after 9/11, when Bush was telling people not to go to the malls and all this kind of stuff, so not many people went to see it. The cast loved everything about the film, and *audiences* loved it when it came out on DVD—where it's become huge—but the country was in such turmoil. Movies can be very important, and I think they're great for our culture, but at the time we were so disoriented, like the rest of the world, we barely remembered that we had even *made* a movie. It was just a very, very dark time for several months there.

Making *Bandits,* though, was just an amazing experience. Other than the bleeding gums and the stress. I loved being with Bruce, Cate, and Troy Garity, who's Jane Fonda's son and plays the fourth member. And Bruce did something for me that I'll never forget.

I had just come back from England, where I had been visiting Angie on the first *Tomb Raider,* and I had to go to New York and hang out with Matt Damon and Penélope Cruz to do some press. Then I went to Chicago and did *The Oprah Winfrey Show* with Matt. I think I had just recently finished *The Man Who Wasn't There* and was about to go into *Bandits,* but when I got back to L.A. I had horrible pain, just like I did in '84, and ended up in the hospital with God knows what and weighing nothing. I had no electrolytes, no potassium, just like I did in 1984. I was in the hospital for about ten days, and the movie company just wanted to move on and find somebody else, but Bruce wanted me for his partner in *Bandits* to start with, so he told those guys he was not making the movie without me. When they asked, "Well, how long do we wait for him?" Bruce just said, "However long it takes." I'll never forget him for that.

I don't hang out with actors a lot, but let me tell you something, there have been guys—*real* friends *who happen to be* in the entertainment business—who have stood up for me. People who I'll never forget.

※

Boxmasters, Continental Club, Austin, Texas. J.D., me, Mike Butler.
Photograph © by Van Redin.

Playing drums on "A Fool for Your Stockings," Fort Worth, Texas. ZZ Top drummer Frank Beard enjoys a break. *Photograph courtesy of J.D. Andrew.*

Onstage in Salina, Kansas. *Photograph courtesy of J.D. Andrew.*

Same show. By the second half of shows, the suits come off and we get louder.
Photograph courtesy of J.D. Andrew.

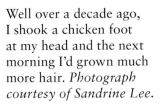

Well over a decade ago, I shook a chicken foot at my head and the next morning I'd grown much more hair. *Photograph courtesy of Sandrine Lee.*

Then just a few years back, I shook an entire chicken at myself and my hair returned to its original color. Even darker. Unfortunately, it also gave Brad Davis hemorrhoids. *Photograph courtesy of Aymeric Montouchet.*

Me and J.D. at Shannon's in St. Louis with Bobby Knight, Tony La Russa, and Jim Leyland. These guys are the real thing.

Ritchie "Cat Daddy" Montgomery, me, J.P. Shellnut, and J.D. Andrew on the set of *Baytown Disco.* J.D.'s bleeding ulcer evident in this photo. *Photograph courtesy of Lynne Eagan.*

With Tom Epperson getting lunch packed for work during Tom's visit to Georgia.
Photograph courtesy of Connie Angland.

Coming home from location scout for *Jayne Mansfield's Car. Photograph courtesy of Connie Angland.*

Bella and me. Beauty and the Beast, thank goodness her mom's pretty. *Photograph courtesy of Connie Angland.*

Connie and Bella in their '60s getups in Cedar Town, Georgia, first day of *JMC*. *Photography © by Van Redin.*

First assistant director Jim Hensz, me, Duvall, Cedar Town. Here's how I direct Bobby. "That's great, Bobby!" *Photography © by Van Redin.*

Planning a shot in Cedar Town. (Left to right) camera assistant Steve Search, cinematographer Barry Markowitz, me, Jim Hensz, and script supervisor Anne Rapp, headless, holding script. She does very good work regardless of the no-head thing. *Photography © by Van Redin.*

Two Beauties and the Beast. On the first day of *JMC. Photography © by Van Redin.*

In director uniform on set of *JMC*, La Grange, Georgia. *Photography © by Van Redin.*

Mom with Kevin Bacon on *JMC* set. They later married. My stepdad's an actor. Cool.

Bella, proud of a grasshopper on her arm on the set of *JMC*. *Photograph courtesy of Connie Angland.*

At endangered frog
aquarium with Bobby
Duvall. *Photograph
courtesy of
Connie Angland.*

One of the great
pleasures of my life, a
walk with Bella.
*Photograph courtesy
of Connie Angland.*

Can't deny this rascal. Me and my son Willie, I think 2009. *Photograph courtesy of Connie Angland.*

Christmas at home, 2010. Me, niece Ginny, Mom, Bella, Willie. *Photograph courtesy of Connie Angland.*

With Dan Lanois at the Cave in mid-interview. *Courtesy of Keisha Kalfin.*

My boys Willie, eighteen, and Harry, seventeen, at home.

Fourth of July, Georgia. Me and the girls with the great John Hurt.

J.D. and I enjoying an adult beverage in Atlanta.

Bella playing a video game, Connie talking to Tom E. The other two guys are just morons.

My son Willie was four months old when our house in Los Flores Canyon—the first real house I ever had, I hadn't bought it yet, we were just leasing it, but I was thinking about buying it—burned to the ground in the big Malibu fire of '93. We lost everything we had. Pietra—Willie's and my son Harry's mom—and I went over to my studio, to the dressing room at CBS, and slept in there for the first night. It was the only place we had to go. The next day we went to the Sheraton Universal Hotel, one of the hotels giving cut rates to victims of the fire. We literally watched our house burning on the news. Harry Thomason and Linda Bloodworth-Thomason—who were the producers of *Evening Shade* and *Hearts Afire*, the TV shows I was on—gave us some money, put us up in an apartment, and went with Pietra with a credit card to the clothing store to get clothes for her and Willie. We named Harry, who wasn't born yet, Harry James, for Harry Thomason. James is for my brother Jimmy.

Anyway, other people who have been golden—and this is probably supposed to be part of the acknowledgments page or an awards speech, but I don't care—are John Ritter, Robert Duvall, Bruce Willis, Dennis Quaid, Penélope Cruz, Cate Blanchett, and John Cusack. There's Bruce Dern, with whom I got to do a couple of scenes in *The Astronaut Farmer* and who I consider to be a real legend and a hero of mine. Angie, above all. And I would absolutely be remiss if I didn't mention one of my best friends in the world, Dwight Yoakam, who I think is one of the few people who keeps true to what he does. He's doing the same thing now as he was doing when he first started. I admire that. Dwight and I have had amazing times over the years. Dwight is a great actor, a great songwriter, a great musician, a great singer, and a great friend. I couldn't even go into all the times we've had. Just know that Dwight and I have many stories to tell. I hope he writes a book one day, because he's not lazy like me and he'll probably tell you the whole thing. And he was amazing in *Sling Blade*. So were Jimmy Hampton, Rick Dial, Lucas Black, John Ritter, and Natalie Canerday—they all should've been noticed way more than they were for that movie. I've spent nights hanging out with Dwight, Gary Busey, Kinky Friedman, Bud Cort, and Warren Zevon all at once. Now, think about *that* group.

There have been some really, really good people, so many to name, who have been good to me over the years. Those old directors who took me in and gave me advice early on: Stanley Kramer and Billy Wilder, who I'll owe forever.

I'll always love Matt Damon and Ben Affleck. I knew them back when they were kids running around town. Just good kids. And look at them now.

Fred Roos. Great producer. He was a casting director in the sixties and has been responsible for discovering a lot of people: Harrison Ford, Suzanne Somers, Richard Dreyfuss, Paul Le Mat, just to name a few. And me. Fred, if it weren't for him seeing me in a couple of things in the theater, I don't know what I'd be doing. Joe Byrne, Jeb Rosebrook, producers of *The Outsiders* television show Fred got me in for. My friend Coby and his wife, Katja, who took me in when I was broke and starving and really saved my life. Another great guy, Brad Pitt. Another great guy, George Clooney. These are big movie stars, you know, but I have to tell you, they're regular guys. Kristin Scott has been my assistant for ten years. Bruce Heller was my assistant years ago and became a producer with me, and I owe a great debt of gratitude to him. And also my West Coast Ensemble pals Greg Littman, Forest Witt, Jesse Dabson, Rick Krause, and Tom Chaliss.

These are all people who make a life. If you add them up, the famous ones and the not-famous ones, they're the people that are just the fabric of this life you build out here. Anybody who ever has a bad word to say about any of those people I mentioned, they are full of shit. I can tell you at the end of the day, those are the people that if I needed them they'd be there. I've had assistants, managers, agents, some of them who have been awful, some of them full of shit. Some people you want to slap the piss out of. But I won't go into those folks because I don't think it's good to talk bad about people, I never have. I'll talk bad about types and injustices, not individuals. That's my policy.

CHAPTER FORTY

Angie

They call her Miss Lucky, she was born in a hurricane

The wind blew her down a dark and magic lane

She's a golden gypsy lighting up the way

For anyone who needs her night or day

Her thunder casts a spell in magic tones

Her lightning strikes and courses through your bones

Her power leaves you spent there where you lay

And leaves you trying to find something to say

Beautiful is all that comes to mind

The understatement that seems to me unkind

Beautiful is all that comes to mind

The words just seem to be so hard to find

Her rain comes pouring down to wash you clean

Unless you're in the flood you can't know what I mean

Her power leaves you spent there where you lay

And leaves you trying to find something to say

Beautiful is all that comes to mind

It's hard to even look and not go blind

Beautiful is all that comes to mind

The words just seem to be so hard to find

Beautiful is all that comes to mind

M Y MANAGER GEYER KOSINSKI CALLED ME ONE DAY SOMETIME IN the nineties and said, "I signed this young girl, she's Jon Voight's daughter. She's, like, the female version of you. I desperately want you guys to work together, but I'm afraid to introduce you because I'm afraid you guys will get married."

Angie and I got to be really good friends over the years. We were attracted to each other in the way that's, like, oh yeah, there's that other human being I can relate to. We became closer during *Pushing Tin,* and after the movie finished shooting we ended up seeing each other.

We later got married in one of those chapels in Las Vegas. I was somewhere in the South, Nashville or somewhere, recording some demos with my buddy Harvey Cook, who was a video playback guy on movies. After we finished recording, we were driving cross-country to get back to Los Angeles when Angie called me and said, "If we're going to get married, we should probably do it right now." And I said, "Yeah, why not?" We had been seeing each other for a while, and we had known each other since she was a kid of nineteen or twenty.

Harvey was our best man because he happened to be right there with me. At the chapel in Las Vegas, there was this woman playing the organ who turned out to be the sister of Jimmie Fadden, the drummer for the Nitty Gritty Dirt Band.

After we were married, we went back to L.A. Angie saw this house that was for sale in Beverly Hills and it had a studio. We looked at different places, but the house we bought together, the one that she wanted, was the one that had a music studio, because she knew I wanted a music studio. That's how she thinks.

The house belonged to Slash, and I saw him at the Sunset Marquis that night and he said, "Hey, I heard you guys came and looked at my house. That's great because I want cool people to own my house." Slash is a great dude.

Angie and I had an amazing time together. We both did a couple of great movies while we were together; I did *The Man Who Wasn't There* and *Monster's Ball,* and she did *Tomb Raider* and *Beyond Borders.* We had the best time, and we had some very good people around us. We were very close. But I always thought I was sort of Quasimodo or the Phantom of the Opera, and when I was with her I think that really reached its heights. I never felt good enough for her, and when you're reading all the nasty, negative comments that people make, it's really hurtful and it's hard to keep a relationship together. Those guys who spread gossip—particularly the writers—don't know what they do to people. Everybody was raised up out of the same stardust, and it gets a little creepy when you're made fun of. We all had that in school. Anyway, I love her dearly, and she's one of my greatest friends no matter what they said years ago in the press. We're great friends and always will be, but that doesn't sell gossip magazines. Good shit doesn't sell and *scandal* does, I guess.

The reason Angie and I split up was because I couldn't take it. Angie, I felt, was definitely too good for me, and at some point, if you believe somebody's too good for you, you're going to mess it up. She and I both know that I messed it up, but the good thing about her is, she doesn't judge me. Never did. I never felt like I was good enough for her, and it had nothing to do with looks. They say, "Well, she's the most beautiful woman in the world and he's an ugly motherfucker." That was never a problem, because women don't look at men the same way men look at women. Any guy could be Robert Redford if a woman thinks he's cool enough. Women got the short end of the stick with that deal. A man could run into a woman who might be the smartest person who ever lived, funny and everything else, but if she looks like she has a foot for a face, he probably won't go there unless he's real drunk, it's real late, and she's the only one around. It's not fair of us, but it's just part of our shitty natures.

There weren't any hard feelings when Angie and I split up. Believe it or not, she actually did like me, and that's the story that I'll tell because the rest of it is none of anybody's business. Even now, anytime the press says anything bad about her, I get real mad. They actually have the gall to criticize her for doing what she does out in the world. They'll say, "Oh, here she goes again, how many more kids is she going to adopt?" Well, what's wrong with that? They're really stretching when they say something bad about her. I guess it makes sense that some cretin is going to attack somebody who's beautiful and smart and talented. That must be where it comes from.

I'm proud of the way she's handled having a family. She's great for Brad, Brad's great for her. I'm with Connie, who I love. Angie and Brad are doing great. I support them 100 percent. I'm right where I need to be, and she's right where she needs to be. She and I are still real close, but we keep our friendship to ourselves. It's sacred. Angie is a little girl and a woman and a teenager and a ghost all wrapped up in one. She deserves everything. She deserves the best. If that's not what the dirt-mongers want to hear, then fuck them. It's the damn truth.

CHAPTER FORTY-ONE

My Term as Mayor of the Sunset Marquis

THE SUNSET MARQUIS HOTEL IS SORT OF MY HAVEN, MY SPIRITUAL home in a way. It's my favorite hotel in the world. It doesn't really *look* like a hotel. It's nestled there in West Hollywood, kind of out of the way of everything.

I started staying there in the nineties. The place had all these great Jim Marshall photographs up everywhere; Jim Marshall was a rock-and-roll photographer who took all these famous, iconic pictures of people like Johnny Cash, Waylon Jennings, Janis Joplin, the Stones, and just about everybody else. He's the one who took that amazing black-and-white picture of Johnny Cash shooting the finger.

The bar at the Sunset Marquis was called the Whiskey Bar, which we used to close down on a regular basis. The guy who ran the bar, Wendell (he's since passed away), was a great dude. It was like hanging out at your own house, in your own living room. Everybody came there. The place is a little more tame these days because I think *everything* is in some ways. The eighties and nineties and into the early 2000s when I stayed there, it was pretty wide-open.

The waitresses at the Whiskey Bar all wore these catsuits, and on a scale of one to ten, they were all ten-plus. Sometimes at the end of the night Wendell would just close the bar and lock the door and I'd sit there talking to him for hours. Maybe a couple of the waitresses would stick around while they were cleaning up. We just had an amazing time.

Dwight wanted to make a video and write a song about the Sunset Marquis. The video would start with this limousine pulling up, and then you'd see these boots getting out of the limousine. The camera would stay on the boots, and in the frame you would see a bag swinging along. The camera would follow the boots as they walked into a hallway, across a marble floor, and up to a desk, where they would stop. Then you'd hear a woman say, "Welcome back, Mr. Thornton." The camera would pan up, and you'd see the bag in my hand and me standing there checking into the Sunset Marquis again.

The standard joke is that every time I would get a divorce I would stay at the Sunset Marquis (that is to say, pretty often). In the beginning, I used to go there just to hang out with people, so a lot of my friends from my years in L.A. have been guys I've met over at the old Whiskey Bar.

I actually lived at the Marquis for a total of about six years. The first time I lived there for a period of two and a half years in Villa 4 North. During another stretch I lived there for a year and a half in 2 South. Later on I lived there for two more years. This was in the nineties, part of 2000, and a little bit in 2001. When Angie and I first got married, we didn't have any place to live, so we lived there. After we bought our first house, the one I'm still in now, we stayed at the Marquis while we got the house redone.

The thing about the Marquis is that it's mainly the *music* hotel. There *were* some actors who stayed there—quite a few

British actors, actually—actors who I go way back with, such as John Hurt, who's in the movie I just did, *Jayne Mansfield's Car,* and Gabriel Byrne. Richard Harris lived below me for a while. I had some great times with those guys. But at any given time it looked just like the Rock and Roll Hall of Fame over there.

When I lived in Villa 4 North, Keith Richards was right below me. Chris Robinson lived in my building when Kate Hudson first started seeing him. There was Deana Carter, the guys from Metallica, the guys from Aerosmith, guys from U2, Dale Bozzio from Missing Persons with, like, eleven different colors of hair and cooler than shit. There were all kinds of music people staying there.

After I split up with their mom, I saw my sons Willie and Harry on the weekends, Friday through Sunday. They were three and four years old, and they would come stay with me at the Marquis. I remember times that my kids were swimming in the pool with other kids whose dads were in Metallica and other bands. I remember one time in particular sitting out there watching my kids swimming while Kirk, Lars, and James Hetfield from Metallica were all sitting around the pool doing the same thing. Willie used to get throwaway cameras and chase Lars around the back lawn all the time and say, "I'm going to get a picture of your butt, Lars!" Lars used to wear these silk shorts all the time, and Willie would chase Lars around trying to take pictures of his ass. I still have some snapshots of just Lars's ass and these silk shorts, most of them without his face in them so I can't really use them against him. Those were some good times when I had my sons there.

One time Jimmy Page, who was staying at the Sunset Marquis, sent me a card that said something like, "I really dig your movies, I'm a big fan." I was like, "Wow! Fucking Jimmy Page!"

He's a legendary guy to me. So I sent him something, I think it was a bottle of champagne. Later on I was doing sit-ups on the floor of this little gym they had in the same building as my villa when all of a sudden I'm looking up some cat's big khaki shorts and there's this little boy standing next to him holding his hand. It's Jimmy Page. He's like, "Hey, mate, thanks for the champagne," and I just kind of froze. There I was, lying on the floor, talking to Jimmy Page. We had about a ten-minute conversation, and I never got off my back. I just lay there on the floor of the gym talking to Jimmy Page. After he left, I was like, *Did I just lie on my back in the fucking gym here and have a conversation with Jimmy Page?* That was astounding.

During the time I lived there, I had been nominated for quite a few awards. I would go to the awards ceremonies, and then, win or lose, I'd be right back at the Marquis, where they would sometimes have after-parties. These days I'm so agoraphobic that I'm really hesitant to get out of the house, but back in those days I didn't *have* to get outside the house. The parties just came there. It was a busy, amazing place.

I became, like, the mayor of the Sunset Marquis, and to this day it's the only place I can go in public where I feel protected. I get the same feeling there that I had at my grandmother's house back in Arkansas. They make everybody that stays there feel like it's their own home. They don't let the paparazzi hang around on the street out front, and they don't *ever* let people inside who are going to be harassing you. I got to know the people who work there, the housekeepers, the security guys. It's like a family. They're very protective.

Today when you walk into the lobby, there's a huge picture of me on one side and a huge picture of Slash on the other side. They've changed the pictures out. It used to be Willie Nelson,

Kris Kristofferson, the Allman Brothers, the Doors, Janis Joplin. Now it's given way to the next guard at that hotel: me, Slash, other cats like that.

I still run in to people there every now and then, good friends like Jed Leiber, a great songwriter/musician whose dad was from Leiber and Stoller, the famous songwriting duo; and Jeff Barry, a great songwriter. I run into those kinds of people there, and it's as close as it gets, for me, to being part of something like the Rat Pack or whatever, because that's kind of what we were. I made a lot of great friends at the Sunset Marquis. It was just its own world over there. I wish there were more places like it.

CHAPTER FORTY-TWO

"Game of Shadows"

There was a time
When I walked the streets
Just like anyone
But something in my
Head turned me
Into a setting sun
Now every time I get the call
To walk inside the outside walls
I know I'll have to play
The game of shadows

—"Game of Shadows" (Thornton/Davis)

GOSSIP USED TO BE FOR WOMEN AT THE BEAUTY SHOP WHEN THEY'D talk about what the neighbor did. It was just something to do. Now gossip has become a multibillion-dollar business, and that's kind of what's changed entertainment for everyone.

As I alluded to earlier, I've had some pretty bitter divorces and other stuff over the years, and there were some people that said awful things about me in the papers. I accept that the press is so wrong most of the time, but unless it happens to *you,* you might have no idea *how completely wrong* a story can be. You give the press one little thing, and they blow it up into a mess. When I talked about my phobias, the story evolved into my being a vampire who lived in a dungeon, drank blood, bit women on the neck, and sucked their blood. None of it was true. I've always had a blood thing, so there's a possibility that I might be reincarnated from a vampire, but I'm not one—certainly not in *this* lifetime.

Here's an example of how the press took something and twisted it into a whole different thing. Angie and I gave each other a necklace with a little, clear locket. It wasn't a vial of blood, as the legend has it. A vial is what you do chemistry experiments in. These weren't test tubes, these were little lockets, but by the time the press was done with us, they had us both walking around with flower vases full of blood around our necks. That wasn't the case at all, far from it. The truth is, Angie and I poked ourselves in the finger and rubbed it all over a glass locket. It was a drop of blood on a locket. From that, in the public eye, we became Bela Lugosi, Nosferatu, and the whole vampire mafia. The press always thought she had all these weird traits, and that I did too.

But I wasn't agoraphobic or paranoid until I found out exactly how many people on the Internet don't like me for whatever reason. Nowadays, you don't need facts to be right, you just have to be the first person to get the first word in. So if somebody says you're a prick publicly, people believe you're a prick, it doesn't even matter what you say after, and even if it's proven later that the guy who *said* you're a prick is actually the prick, you're still a prick forever. There's still going to be that thing in people's heads, and that's who you are for the rest of your life. Until the Internet, I never knew that shit.

Today, mostly what I do when I'm not working is play with my daughter, Bella, hang out with my sons, Willie and Harry, or go to the market with my girlfriend, Connie. When I'm not doing those things—or working, of course—I watch the History Channel or the Military Channel. I also like ESPN or Fox Sports, having grown up as an obsessed athlete and sports fan. But I really don't get out of the house much. I have actually become kind of a shadow, because people can't get me out of the bunker anymore. Not very often anyway. I wrote a song about it called "Game of Shadows." But here's the thing, the people who go, "Hey, man, I love you, can I get a picture?" are the same ones who get on the Internet and say things about me. They love you and they hate you. It's always been like that, but this whole computer generation. . . . And that's why entertainment is being ruined. Now, this is not a slam on my fans. As an entertainer, I want to have a lot of fans, but the fact of the matter is, my fans will always be the same ones. I'm never gonna be *the* guy who makes a movie that will make $500 million. I've been *in* some of those, but so was somebody else. I was in *Armageddon*—that made a shitload of money, but it's not because of me. It's because of the people who made it, the way they made it, and the audience to which it was directed.

But *art* is being ruined because of what we finally did. This is how we're moving through life. People blame it on the system. They blame the movie studio, the record label, the corporations. They say corporations are doing a lot of horrible shit to us, that they're killing us and ruining the world. And they *are*, but not the way you may think. What corporations are, what studios are, are places that make money. They don't give a fuck whether they have to kill you or blow you or come over and play Monopoly with you and your kids all night long. If it makes them money, they really don't give a shit.

For years, guys like me have been whining and bitching about the corporations and the studios and the labels, and, well, here's where it went wrong. It went wrong when the corporations figured out that they could make the people think *they* run things by preying on on their weaknesses. To make them *think* they have a voice. When I was growing up, we had the slogan "Power to the people." Well, *this* ain't what we meant. This is just not what we meant. We were talking about fighting the government. We didn't mean let every asshole on earth dictate what we do as artists or how we live our lives. We meant, let's not let the system and the government work us, let's not let people get killed in a useless war over oil, money, territory, power, religion, whatever they're fighting over. That's what we meant. We didn't mean let Norman from Des Moines, Iowa, get on CNN and Twitter and tell the world what he thinks about the oil spill. We didn't mean *that*.

This Twittering shit has really got to stop. Once in a blue moon I'll watch the news just because I always kind of have faith—faith that somehow I'll turn on the news just to find out that yes, there's going to be a tornado in Georgia, or no, there won't be. That's all I want to know. But I put the news on and find out that there's been a congressman, a Congressman Weiner, who sent a picture of his wiener to somebody. Instead of just reporting on it, the newscaster asks the viewers what they think about it. And then you get someone telling you, on the crawl, what they think about Weiner. "I think he's terrible. I can't believe he showed his wiener." Are you high? That's what this society has become? Show me a politician who hasn't slept with some assistant and I'll show you a eunuch.

When we said "Power to the people," we didn't mean "Let's

listen to somebody in a pair of stretch pants in the middle of the country and see what they have to say on their blog." We didn't mean "I'm going to make a movie that's about some horrible shit I went through in my life and we're going to let the audience tell me how to end the thing."

People don't understand that this system we currently live in has made the people think *they are* the system. And I guess they are now. We've given people too much power. We've given the people these crazy ideas—iPhones, iChat, I do this, I do that, my thing, my this, my that—and created these gadgets to make everyone think *they* are important. And it's killing our society. All of a sudden, everyone from the most intelligent human in the world to the funniest guy to the most talented guy all the way to a blithering idiot are equal because they all have a goddamn Facebook. I spent twenty-five years trying to get out of the woods and I finally did, and then I spent another twenty-five years trying to *not see* these people who tortured me my whole life again, and you think I want a Facebook so they can find me? Are you fucking kidding me? I don't get it. I don't understand the whole concept of it, but I do know this: people who feel that they're not important enough *love* it. And they're being hoodwinked. Anytime you want you can punch in a few buttons and watch people hurt themselves, fall down, and puke, and celebrities eat a cheeseburger on the patio and pass out, or whatever it is. And the Facebook people all get to write each other—they've got this secret society.

I really didn't know how many people hated me until I saw the Internet. Before, we were blind to whoever hated us. If I made a movie and put it out there, I'd see some reviews that were lukewarm or bad or great, but they were done by critics, and for me it was okay, because that's what they were. They've studied movies, they love movies, sometimes I agreed with these critics, sometimes I disagreed, but they had some goddamn right to do it. Once you let any son-of-a-bitch in the world become a critic, all of a sudden there are people all over the place saying, "Why is this motherfucker making another movie, fuck him and his crazy ex-wife and his crazy blood-drinking horseshit ways. I wish this son-of-a-bitch would die." Wow. I had no idea I had affected somebody that way. I mean, at the end of the day—you know what it is, and you don't want to hear it, it's somebody who thinks they deserve to be in their own version of my position. But they don't know what my position is *to start with*. My position may be a lot less lofty than they think it is. I came from a horrible situation. I grew up in poverty, got my ass beat, moved out here to California to realize my dreams, only to go and live in poverty some more. I went through a lot of stuff and paid dues forever.

It doesn't feel good to have people talking about you. They think you got so much money. I'm not a rich movie star myself. Some people are, some people aren't. I make really good money, and I appreciate every bit of it, and I appreciate the fact that I get to do what I love. I love movies and I love music, and I always want to do those things. Mainly I love it, though, between "Action" and "Cut"—when you're actually doing it. I think a lot of actors would tell you that, and as a musician, when I'm recording or playing live for people, *that's* when I like it. A lot of the other stuff that goes with it, the gossip, the nasty criticism— we're all still little kids inside, and when people say bad things about you, it cuts you to the bone. Nobody likes to put up with that stuff, and they say you got to, that it's all part of your job. You're a public figure. But is it really a part of your job? To be cut to shreds all the time? When all you're doing is what you love and you're trying to do it for people? Like I said, I don't make a lot of money in movie-business terms. In music, I don't make *any*. In fact, I go broke doing it, but I love it.

Believe me, once you get out here and you get in this and you have some kids and some ex-wives, the problems are the same, and you end up suddenly being in debt, and you may have to do a movie that you don't particularly want to because you need the money. If you only knew how it works inside, and you knew the people and some of the horrible shit we deal with and what it does. On top of that, to be a performer, you have to have some kind of ego to start with, and let me tell you, they can cut it to shreds instantly. So we certainly don't need the fans helping out, because we get plenty of that out here within the business. It's been a real long hard road, and I've been doing it for thirty years.

And I *do* appreciate the fans. I have a lot of fans. Not as many as I wish I did, but I've got quite a few for not being one of the top five guys. It really gets to you when you work really hard to do something. See, I didn't get handed this. My dad wasn't a movie producer. I spent a life of poverty and living from hand to mouth to get this stuff going. It's been a great thing for me, but people don't understand how taxing it is and how your life becomes this open book, and not even the truth. It's whatever anybody says.

At the end of the day, I can still say I've done some movies and some records that I'm very proud of, and I know we did them the way we wanted to and they came out with the original vision intact. That's all you can hope for. These days, if we get to make a movie that ends up the way we thought it would or hoped it would, then I'm happy with it no matter what anybody else thinks about it. We really do love the fans that we have and try to ignore all the negative stuff as much as we can, but making the actual movie, too, can be very hard.

This summer we made *Jayne Mansfield's Car,* and I have to tell you, it was 105 degrees and I was in charge of some pretty big classic actors who I had to deal with every day. I had to make sure that everybody was happy *and* be in the movie myself. It's a big responsibility. I got real sick down there. I didn't know if I would make it through the movie. It's that weight. People who haven't done it say, with sarcasm, "Oh, getting to be a movie star and being on a movie set is hard." Well, you have to come do it or you'll never know. I know what it's like to be a carpenter because I've been one. I've worked at a sawmill, I've worked at a screen-door factory, I've worked at a machine shop, I've hauled hay, I grew up doing all that stuff. I do know what that's like and how hard it is. But being a filmmaker is hard too. You take on this responsibility to get up at five in the morning and work for eighteen to nineteen hours a day for up to five months and know that you have to be good.

Now, not everybody has that particular talent. You can get better (or even a little worse) at it with experience and depending on who you listen to, but I think you're either born to be an actor or you're not. It's like being a professional athlete. Those guys that can toss a basketball through a hoop, or hit a 98-mile-per-hour fastball the way they do, with that sort of skill, and *especially* those guys who play football and are risking their lives—why *don't* they deserve the money? I do think agents have ruined sports in a lot of ways and that advertising companies have caused resentment among people—there are definitely times when I instinctively say, "They're going to pay that guy *how* much money?" But "professional athlete" is a very short career, and a lot of the people that actually make it don't have the opportunity to continue on as announcers or get big endorsement deals afterward. So they get what they can *while* they can. Of course, as an actor, you can be doing your thing until you're eighty because you're not *actually playing* football. But think about how often careers go downhill. So there may be a very small window in your career as a big actor where you could make some money. It could be ten years. It could be *two* years. But the point is, you have a talent to act and you love it, so you go out there and do it for as long as you can. And of course, as an entertainer, you *want* it to be good and you *want* people to like it. You *want* devoted fans, and you *want* to keep a great business and a great culture alive. I try to make good movies. Maybe I don't all the time, but I'm not *trying* to make a shitty movie or write a shitty book or make shitty music just so I can fuck people. I love it and I want you to love it too. That pressure alone is emotionally draining. A lot of times we do very physical movies, and then it becomes *physically* draining as well. Sure, I've been mad at my profession sometimes. I've said I didn't like it because I was envious that I wasn't really getting to do what some other people were getting to do. We've all had that at some point, where your job becomes hard on your inside and consequently hard on your relationships. Now imagine a job as precarious as acting, directing, and writing.

A lot of the reasons actors get paid money is because big companies that make big movies have a lot of money. I *have,* at certain times, made big money too, but not anymore, given the fact that most movies now are about naked teenage vampires or models with gladiator suits on or video-game movies. So for guys like me who are in their fifties and older—and even guys who are in their forties—it's hard to get a movie financed, and we don't make the same money as we used to, even as little as five years ago. It's especially difficult for women because they want to throw them out the door after thirty sometimes.

These days, if you want to make a real movie, they pay you nothing for it. Actors work for scale all the time. I've done it many times. The independent films I've done, I don't take money up front for them. I get it on the back end, meaning, I take a chance right along with everyone else. If it's successful, you make some money. If it fails, you don't get any. Most of the movies I'm known for were like that. Of the movies I *have* been paid big money for, some of them made money, some of them didn't, but as I said, I wasn't supposed to carry most of them myself.

But I don't really know anybody out there who, if somebody offered them a certain amount of money for doing anything—fixing toilets, doing a movie, whatever—would say, "Oh no, I don't want to do that, I'm so Zen about everything, I don't care about money." Sure, there are people like that in the world, but they live on the top of a mountain someplace. People certainly line up to win the lottery, and that doesn't take any talent, that takes *luck*.

CHAPTER FORTY-THREE

The Ballad of the Alamo

BECAUSE OF TOO MUCH ACCESS, WE NOW HAVE NO HEROES. WE'LL never have heroes again like Elvis Presley, the Beatles, Jerry Lee Lewis, Jimmy Stewart, and Marlon Brando. When we saw Jimmy Stewart, Paul Newman, Steve McQueen, or Ava Gardner, the only time we saw them was on the screen. Not scratching their ass walking down the street on YouTube. I'm not saying there will never be somebody who's hugely *famous* again. There will be plenty of those motherfuckers. I'm saying we won't have magical heroes.

I mean great people who have done truly great things. And I don't just mean actors and musicians, either. One of the things in my career of which I'm most proud is playing Davy Crockett, because all those guys at the Alamo were heroes to me. From now on, I can know I played Davy Crockett in *The Alamo* and that will be in cinematic history, you know? John Wayne played him too, but I was told by the historians that we made the most historically accurate movie that's been made about the Alamo— not only in the performances but in John Lee Hancock's treatment of the script.

Some people don't want to hear it that Davy Crockett was executed, but that was in the diary of a Mexican lieutenant who was there, and that's as close as we can get to the truth, so *that's* in the movie. For some reason, people say, "No, Davy Crockett died like in the painting, where he's swinging his rifle and he was the last man standing. He was overrun and killed." I mean, really, what's the difference? When you're shooting those kind of black-powder rifles, those muskets, you got one shot, so if you didn't get reloaded in time, it's completely conceivable that he was just overrun, but when you think about it, if Crockett and his guys were captured, that means they *were* the last ones standing. So Davy Crockett fought to the end and they captured him, and I'm sure as big a name as Davy Crockett had, Santa Anna in particular wanted to be eye-to-eye with him before he killed him. In the Mexican lieutenant's diary, it says that Davy Crockett died with dignity. So that's the way we portrayed it.

John Lee Hancock made a great movie. Jason Patric, Patrick Wilson, Dennis Quaid, and everybody involved, from the production staff to the extras, felt the same way. On top of that, we were based in Austin, Texas, which is my second home. I know everybody in Austin.

I think it didn't do better at the box office because fourteen-year-olds go to movies and fourteen-year-olds don't give a shit about history anymore. I think if the whole movie had been about a battle, it might have been different. But it wasn't. *The Alamo* was about waiting. It was thirteen days there in that fort, and people don't want to watch the waiting-for-thirteen-days. Well, that's not the whole movie, but today's audiences just want to see somebody get stuck with a bayonet and a bunch of shooting. I think if that movie had come out in the seventies, it would have done very well.

CHAPTER FORTY-FOUR

"There's Always Somebody Watchin'"

I can't pee in my bathroom

I can't pee in my yard

Can't get in my house

Can't get past the guard

Can't have an affair

Can't color my hair

'Cause there's always somebody watchin'

—"There's Always Somebody Watchin'"

(Thornton/Andrew)

NOWADAYS YOU CAN BE FAMOUS BECAUSE YOU ATE THE MOST WORMS, or get a record deal because you lost two hundred pounds on television. So what is *fame* anymore? When we were growing up, we would be ashamed if the way we got famous was by winning a talent contest. Nobody ever became the biggest fucking rock star on earth from being on Ted Mack's *The Original Amateur Hour*. Those were people who had a poodle and a kazoo or something. I didn't make it by skateboarding down a banister and landing in a pile of watermelons on YouTube in a minute-and-a-half video. It took well over half my life to get to where I am today.

The fact of the matter is, the audience is now the star.

Reality television shows and TMZ are on major networks now, and the point of these shows is so America can look at stars being ridiculed and made fun of and have cynical things said about them. But it didn't just come along with the computer, it was already happening. What I'm talking about is cynicism. I'm cynical about cynicism. Cynicism has become popular, funny, and entertaining, so in order to combat it, I then have to become cynical about the perpetrators.

This goes back to my thoughts on the loss of heroes. Our children are never going to enter a record store and flip through every record and go, "Oh wow, Dickey Betts, Gregg Allman, Billie Holiday!" or whoever it is, read the liner notes, and get so excited to save up their three dollars and eighty-five cents—yes, ladies and gentlemen, it was three dollars and eighty-five cents for a fucking record album—so they can take it home and play it. You *wanted* to like it. You wanted to like it so fucking bad.

Today I feel like audiences go to movies and buy records to be, like, "Okay, let's see what this motherfucker's done this time." It's like, "Fuck these motherfuckers, I'm going to buy this record and rip it to shreds." As a result, today every cartoon you see on TV, every TV show practically, is mean-spirited and de-signed to cut somebody to pieces. And it's *funny* to people.

When people go to a movie today, some random person with a blog will point something out about it, and then the next thing you know that becomes the thing every article is about. "Did you notice how the continuity was horrible in that movie?" When I was growing up, we didn't care. We went and saw a movie, and if we liked it we liked it, and if we didn't like it we didn't like it. Now we live in a society that drives artists inward, and so the real artists do not have the inclination to keep doing their art.

They're afraid of getting their hearts broken. That's what happened to *me* anyway.

The point is, when the audience is so critical of the people who are still making the movies or making the records or writing the books or painting the pictures, they're hurting entertainment, they're hurting art, and they're hurting themselves, mainly because they're never going to feel that magical thing we felt when we were growing up.

I challenged this girl one time who was arguing with me saying I was some kind of dinosaur. I said, "Here's an experiment for you. Take a sheet of paper and, starting with about 1980, write down all the songwriters, singers, and bands who, one hundred years from now, will be in the books as being incredible legendary performers or songwriters. Write them down." She started throwing out names like Michael Jackson and Bruce Springsteen, and I said, "No, you can't count them because they started out in the late sixties. I'll give you REM and U2, because I'm trying to give you *something*. I'll just say, if you take a sheet of paper and, starting at about 1975 and going back to the turn of the century, write down names, you don't have enough paper in your house to write them all down." There's something to that.

I ain't no dinosaur and I ain't acting like my daddy. My daddy didn't like the Beatles because my daddy came from a long line of Irish sawmill workers who were, you know, rednecks and shit, but they were all fairly well educated and came from a time when there wasn't any child abuse—that didn't exist as we know it. You messed something up, you got your ass beat with a razor strap, period. I had mine beat many times. If I made too much noise when he was on the graveyard shift when he worked in a factory, he'd fly through the room in the middle of the day and just beat the living dog shit out of me. That's where I come from, and he came from something even worse than that, and his daddy came from something even worse than that.

When the Beatles came along, do you think my dad was going to like the Beatles? He didn't care if they were good or bad, he wouldn't have known it. My dad didn't even *like* music. My dad was the only person I ever knew who actually didn't like music. It's not that he didn't like rock and roll—he didn't like *music*. Actually, no, he liked two songs: "Easter Parade" and "Puff, the Magic Dragon." Those are the only two songs my dad liked. I'll never know why. One's from a musical, and the other one was supposedly about smoking reefer sung by a folk trio. My dad didn't give a fuck about Peter, Paul, and Mary. If my dad ever ran into them, he'd beat their ass right in the street.

My dad didn't like the Beatles because they were threatening to him, because they were young, nice-looking boys who were playing this strange outer-space music he didn't know anything about, and it didn't have anything to do with working or foot-ball or anything like that. He didn't like them, but not because he thought, *Oh, look at those simple lyrics, "If I fell in love with you would you promise to be true*." He just didn't like them and went about his business liking *other* stuff.

Armchair critics have always been there, tearing apart lyrics like they know something though they've never written a song, and tearing apart a movie though they've never made a movie. Generally these guys are envious or jealous of the motherfucker who made it. But why did we not know about these guys before about ten years ago? Because of *that* fucking thing—that fuck-ing computer right there. It's like, "We're gonna let everybody in the world have one of these machines here, and we're gonna let every one of you call yourself whatever you want to call yourself.

You are an Internet critic, you are a blogger, you have a title, you're *somebody*."

So, I'm just going to say I'm a research scientist. I'm going to tell everyone I'm a theoretical physicist. If some drooling idiot sitting in his basement writing reviews can call himself a legitimate movie critic, I'm going to start calling myself a theoretical physicist, and I'm going to say, "It's my theory if I go outside to my swimming pool right now, stare at it long enough, and throw a softball in it, the United States Senate will appear on my lawn." That makes me a theoretical physicist. We've let anyone call themselves whatever they want to call themselves, and the scary thing is that people listen to them and they're missing all the goddamn magic in life because of it.

Having said all that, I want to point out a cat like Harry Knowles. I know him, he's a good dude. He was a kid in Texas who started his little Ain't It Cool News, and he used to sneak into screenings, then go put the word out on great movies before they came out. He's a critic on the Internet, but Harry is a great guy who loves movies and wanted to spread the word about movies that maybe not everybody would see. Unwittingly, he was like Sam Peckinpah, the first guy to show blood squirting out of people in slow motion. That spawned a lot of bad blood-squirting movies, but Peckinpah did great ones. The problem is, every motherfucker with drool running out of his mouth is a critic. They're not all Harry Knowleses, but they think they are. That's how that shit happened.

I've always wished that critics were people who just talked about what they liked so they could present it to the people; it's like, "Hey, you may not have heard this, and I think you should check it out," as opposed to writing about stuff they *don't* like so they can sound clever and cynical. I don't even know why you would waste your time. If you don't like it, don't worry about it. It's just like a "punish honk" in traffic. People want to punish *now*. We grew up just wanting to love everything, and if you didn't, you simply didn't pay much attention to it. To these so-called critics on the Internet, it's not your sole responsibility in life to warn the public about this dreadful thing that's going to make your ears bleed or your eyes burst. Is that what you really think? That you have a responsibility to the public to protect them from this horror? It just seems weird to me, and it's a slap in the face to real critics.

I'm not saying that good critics don't exist anymore. There *are* some terrific critics out there, and there are even some good ones that do it on the Internet. People who know what they're talking about, so it's kind of a slap in their faces because they've been doing this for a long time. They were *there* back in the day, and their profession is being watered down because of jealous hacks.

Bob Geldolf came on some TV show, I think it was *Craig Ferguson,* who I happen to really love—he kind of takes the piss out of people and society in general—and right in the middle of J.D. and I writing this rock opera about this very subject, Bob said, "Does nobody understand that this is an emergency? Why is nobody saying we're turning into a bunch of morons?" He actually said it. And Craig Ferguson said, "Yeah," and the audience cheered. If you bring people together and say this stuff, they cheer you too, and yet they keep doing the very thing they seemed to agree in the moment they're not supposed to be doing. Nobody with any power is saying this. *I* don't have any power, but maybe someone who does will put an end to this shit someday.

CHAPTER FORTY-FIVE

I Don't Hate Canada

Honey, don't buy what you saw on TV
I know it's got a lifetime guarantee
But when it falls to pieces you're gonna see
Why handling and shipping it ain't free
Folks don't watch the news and expect to find
Anything important or anything of use
Walter Cronkite died on July 17th Oh-Nine
His memory is buried under gossip and abuse
Welcome to Justice
Welcome to fair trade
Welcome to the memory of when we had it made

—"Welcome" (Thornton/Andrew)

FORGIVE ME WHILE I CLEAR THE AIR HERE. MAYBE YOU CARE ABOUT this story, maybe you don't, but I had this incident happen in Canada when we were touring, opening for Willie Nelson, and it's gotten completely out of control because of the Internet. Basically, a guy on the radio up there didn't do a very simple thing that we asked him to *please* do for us, before the interview, on air. So when he'd ask me a question, I wouldn't play his game.

One way or the other, all of a sudden we got like millions of hits or whatever on the fucking Internet because supposedly I went crazy.

To me it wasn't a big deal, but now supposedly I'm some Canada hater. I've always been a Canadian supporter and done movies in that country. A lot of my friends are from Canada. Montreal is like my favorite city in the world, I love that city. But the next thing you know, I'm some asshole who doesn't like Canadians when the truth is, I took exception to *a* Canadian. I wouldn't give a shit if he's from Topeka, Kansas. I was just shocked that was actually news. I love Canada.

See, if it was only newspapers and magazines now, it would've never been news. That a guy got pissed off at a radio guy and wouldn't answer his questions is news enough to get five million hits on the goddamn Internet? Are you serious? But now it's important to people to find out what star shit himself in a restaurant yesterday.

CHAPTER FORTY-SIX

My New Year's Resolution: Try to Calm the Fuck Down

What a good life
I've made here
But what I really miss tonight
Is a smoke and a beer

—"The Good Life" (Thornton/Andrew)

THINK THE WHOLE SMOKING THING IS A WITCH HUNT. YOU CAN'T smoke in West Hollywood anymore. You *cannot* smoke in West Hollywood, California, in the United States of America. You can't even smoke in certain places in Dublin and Paris—cities where *all they do* is smoke. I've been to some of those places, and goddamn, smoking is like their life, and all of a sudden it's banned. Well, I never smoked a cigarette and had a head-on collision. But I've seen motherfuckers drink half a bottle of bourbon and do just that, and there's a liquor store on every corner.

What happened in L.A. was they *decided* that smoking is the number-one killer of everybody. "Well, look at the sign over there in Westwood," they point out. "It says, SMOKING DEATHS

THIS MINUTE: 852 BILLION." How the fuck do they *know* that? What *I* know is, I know a guy who smokes from the time he gets up in the morning to the time he goes to sleep. He also drinks tequila all day long. I saw him not too long ago, and God bless him, he's eighty-some-odd years old and still going. I'm not saying, "Hey, kids, run out and smoke," that's not my point. I'm saying, if I want to smoke outside in a town that I live in, in a town I pay taxes in, I should be able to. If you want to talk about instant death, just mix people and cars with liquor stores and payday. When those guys came up with this smoking ban, did they really think it through all the way? Let's say that during their committee meeting they voted to ban smoking in West Hollywood. To celebrate their new law, they decide to go out and have a cocktail party that night. Now, let's say two hundred of them are at the party. One hundred ninety-eight of those motherfuckers are so drunk they can hardly get out the door after the cocktail party. And then, still hypothetically speaking, let's say eight are in an accident that night and four people die in those eight accidents. Not one person at the cocktail party smoked a cigarette, but four people died. They're not banning liquor, though, are they? I don't think so.

Our band has played a few charity gigs for the American Whatever Association, and we were onstage playing for a room of like five or six hundred shit-faced doctors. They're drunk off their asses, but for some reason, smoking is bad. Those doctors tell us, "You've got to quit smoking," and they quote that sign in Westwood—852 billion or something died from cigarette smoke. They say, "It's true. We've proven it."

Have they proven it? I bet if somebody dug into the AMA hard enough, they would also prove that there's been a cure for cancer and AIDS for a long fucking time, and they won't tell anybody because if they did, their business is over. Can you imagine if there was a car made that never fucking needed a repair and it never broke down? You got one car the rest of your fucking life and it can fly and do your dishes and shit like that? Never has a problem? Can you imagine the automotive industry? Do you think they'd want you to know about that car? You think the oil companies want everybody to drive a fucking electric car? Of course not. And doctors, you go to an orthopedic surgeon and tell him your shoulder hurts, and he'll cut your fucking arm off. But you go to the holistic guy, and he'll say, "Why don't you chew on this sassafras root twice a day." Then, on the other hand, you go to one of *those* cats and they'll muscle-test you by giving you a bottle with nothing in it and a label on it that says BLACK PEPPER. They get you to hold it in your hand, and they test to see if they can put your arm down when you're trying to hold your arm stiff. If your arm goes down, it means you're allergic to black pepper or something. Who the fuck knows if that means anything? I know *one* thing: if you *do* get your arm cut off at a fucking sawmill, *don't* go to a holistic doctor, go right to the horrible pricks who want to cut you to pieces, because they're the only ones who know how to sew it back on.

It's real confusing about these doctors, but I'd suggest to everyone, if you get the chance, go see both of them. Go to those fucking underhanded guys, the so-called real doctors, if you've got an amputated limb or a stomach with a hole in it. If it's just some weird shit and you're not quite sure what it is—you're tired, no energy—go see the alternative doctors because they're not going to just dope you up right away. The drug companies, they really want you to take their medication, and then this is what happens: you take a pill for your arthritis, well, that drives your fucking blood pressure up or down. Now you got to take a fucking blood pressure pill. The blood pressure pill hurts your stomach worse than the arthritis one does, and now you got to take a stomach pill, and so on. They get you hooked on this shit. They've got you on twenty pills all of a sudden, and now, in order to stay alive, you have to keep taking these motherfuckers forever, and every one of them makes you sick so you got to take something to prevent *that* sickness that *that* fucking pill did to you. These pharmaceutical companies want to keep you on dope so bad—you go to a doctor, and they tell you to take seven of these today and twelve of those tomorrow and fifteen of these on Saturday. Then later you see the commercial for this shit, and it says, as I heard on *The Simpsons* one time, "Causes loss of scalp and penis." The commercial will say shit like "increases risk of stroke, heart attack, depression, suicide." You ask them why their drug does all this bad shit, and they'll tell you, "Well, we have to put that on there." Why do you have to put that on there? Because it's happened to people, right? "Well, yeah, but their percentages are very low." Okay, you know what? I don't give a fuck if it's a half a percent. If you happen to be the motherfucker who's in the half percent, that sucks for you. In World War II, the fliers would go out on a bombing run over France or Germany, and they used to say, "You're only on a milk run"—well, it's only a milk run if you make it back. It's not a milk run if your airplane gets shot out of the fucking sky. That's why percentages don't mean shit to me. I've said it before, it's like the weather. There's a 25 percent chance of rain. A 30 percent chance of rain. The fuck does that mean? There's a fifty-fifty chance of everything, all the fucking time. That's the way it is. It's either going to happen or it's not. That's fifty-fifty, so I don't get it—motherfuckers and their percentages. Doctors. Lawyers. What assholes.

So what is it about cigarettes?

"Well, if I have a drink, it doesn't get in the air and bother you."

I'm sitting next to a four-hundred-pound motherfucker who is eating a baked potato the size of a football, with fucking sour cream and butter on it, and a side of steak with more fat on it than you can shake a stick at, and he's got his diet soda there—like that's going to do him any good—and *my* cigarette smoke is going to kill him? When your cholesterol is 319 or some shit like that? Ban butter, you know? It's ridiculous. There's shit out there that will kill you the fuck dead. And maybe smoking will kill *me,* but it's my business if I smoke a cigarette in my fucking alley. I'm sorry. That's my air too. If you're going to say that's not my air, then I'm going to say it ain't that city bus's air either. Let everybody get themselves a wagon and go live in Pennsylvania Dutch Country with the Amish, and then maybe they'll all be real happy because I *guarantee* you there's shit killing you besides me and my little American Spirit cigarette.

I went to this asshole the other day (pardon the pun, and you'll see why in a minute). I decided to get all my medical tests out of the way in January. Sometimes I have to get physicals several times a year because each time you do a movie you have to get a physical for the insurance companies that provide coverage for the production. Every year I try to go do my thing, get my own yearly physical, so this year I went and had the treadmill test with the cardiologist (checked out okay there), went to the dermatologist (everything's fine), went and had my regular physical (no problems). I've had my problems in the past, as I've talked about with the starving-to-death thing, but other than that I've not had much. I've got a little bit of arthritis in my neck, my spine, and my knees because of sports and because of a horse accident years ago that nearly killed me. I had a kidney stone once, which really sucked. Otherwise, I seem to be okay.

I've never had a colonoscopy, and once you get to be fifty you're supposed to go get one, so I asked my doctor if there was a gastroenterologist he could recommend me to see. He said he knew a doctor he thought was good, so I went to him. That doctor—with him it was like *everything* is about "You have to get a colonoscopy." That's the only fucking test you got? He proceeds to scare the shit out of me talking about "We put a tube down your throat and up your ass—we put you out, you don't even know what happened." I was trying to tell him about this problem I've been having with my stomach ever since we were in Atlanta shooting *Jayne Mansfield's Car*. I was just dehydrated all the time, and I think I fucked myself up a little bit.

So there I am, sitting in the exam room, and I'm trying to tell this doctor what's going on with me.

"The problem I've been having is—"

"*I'll ask the questions.*" And he's over there typing while I'm talking. Sometimes doctors want to act like they're fucking God or something. *Well, fuck you and your diploma on the wall. What do you mean you'll ask the questions? If you'll let me tell you for thirty fucking seconds about what's going on, it may give you a clue instead of you asking me all the shit that you know about and seeing what little fucking category it fits in and what test that costs a billion dollars I can take that won't be covered by insurance.* He was a prick. A real asshole. (See? Does the uncalculated pun make sense now?) I was in there for about five minutes before I couldn't stand it. I said, "I had a full body scan recently and an MRI on my head, and they said I'm good."

"You can't tell everything from the scan, or the this or the that . . ."

Well, they can tell if you have a fucking tumor the size of a goddamn grapefruit, which I *don't* have. I went to a fucking blood specialist and got my blood drawn by a guy I know who makes his living as an expert—this is a high-dollar cat who looks for cancer in your blood, and he said I was fine. *All you want to do, because this is your area of expertise, is shove a fucking camera up my ass and that solves every problem in the world. That's the ultimate fucking test you can take.* Okay, fine. I get it. I'm going to get a colonoscopy, goddammit. I've already said, yeah, I was going to do that, but I'm certainly not letting this cold fucking asshole do it. The upshot here is, at the end of the thing he said, "Why would you subject yourself to radiation having a full body scan and yet you eat vegan?"

I said, "Because I fucking want to. *That's* why. I'd like to find out all at once if I've got any bad shit. When somebody's sick in the hospital, you motherfuckers give them that test. You give it to them all the time. As long as you're being paid by the mother-fucker, then you'll give them all the tests you want. But all of a sudden this test is no good. So in other words, you say that your profession is so underhanded that you have a test that's danger-ous to you and it doesn't work. And yet you work in this fucking profession."

I don't trust these cocksuckers. My brother is an RN, and he teaches nursing up in San Jose and San Francisco. He's a really good dude, and he knows that profession inside and out. There are plenty of good people in the medical field, and there are a lot of pricks too. It makes you wonder, *Well, who do I listen to?* You go to the holistic or homeopathic doctor, and they tell you, "Just eat this pill, it's made out of licorice and it will cure you." I've personally found that both of them, the so-called real doctors and the holistic/homeopathic doctors, have a lot of value. If you get your fucking arm cut off, go to the emergency room and let one of those hacks sew your fucking arm back on. But if you're just feeling kind of nervous and you don't understand why you got the shits three times a week and the other four days a week you don't, try a homeopathic or holistic doctor. Get some acupuncture. Because sometimes that shit will fix you up without having these motherfuckers wanting to saw you in half to look at your liver.

My problem is that I'm too nervous and I have physical symptoms *from* being too goddamned worried and nervous all the time. If you can find something, like drink a couple of beers a day—some people like to smoke a joint, and maybe they're better off—maybe that's better than medicine. I'm not condoning drinking *or* dope, I'm just saying. Maybe you just need to do things that will calm you the fuck down, then maybe we wouldn't need doctors so much. That's what I'm working on. It was one of my New Year's resolutions this year. Try to calm the fuck down and not worry so much. Doctors don't want you to calm down.

I know a lot of this is very rambling and angry, but I think it's important. I'm just saying. You're reading words, but there's blood in my eyes.

CHAPTER FORTY-SEVEN

Jayne Mansfield's Car

Come on, kids, gather round

We have a treat for you

If you've never seen it

Then you're long overdue

Observe the twisted metal

Bloodstains and broken glass

We're glad your folks all brought you here

With pockets full of cash

For a dollar you can step inside the rope

You look to me like brave kids who can cope

For two bucks you can stand up on the stage

And look inside the wreck that's all the rage

We travel around the country

To entertain the masses

To show the bloody floorboard

And the scarf and the dark glasses

Come on, folks, step right up

We've traveled oh so far

To let you people have a look

Inside Jayne Mansfield's car

Gaze up at the horror

Tell me what you see
I know it's just a mannequin
But a good facsimile

—"Jayne Mansfield's Car"
(Thornton/Andrew/Butler)

ORWELL WROTE *1984*, WHICH OBVIOUSLY HAD A LOT OF FORESIGHT, but now it's *Revenge of the Nerds*. This whole thing I was saying about the computer—it has become the single most important tool in our society. Cell phones, gadgets, all this kind of shit. Before the computer, you had to be able to run fast, jump high, write a book that said something worth a shit, write a movie, make a record, sculpt something. When I was a little kid, I lived in a place that didn't have movie theaters, so we played with sticks and rocks. When I was about nine years old, I moved into a town that did have a movie theater, and I would be entertained by movies with Don Knotts and Dick Van Dyke because I was a little kid. When I started looking at movies in earnest, when I was probably a teenager, the movies that meant something to me were movies like the original *A Star Is Born* with Fredric March, *A Face in the Crowd*, Elia Kazan's movies. The thing is, they all had something to them. They were movies that were based on something, they had a story to tell, with characters that had something to say. That stuff is no longer important. What's important is that you can sit there and figure out a bunch of shit to bypass all art. The whole experience of going to a movie or going to a concert is lost now. The buildup was as fun as the experience; it was exciting, and when you finally got there, to the movie theater or the concert venue, you listened and you watched and you loved it. To anticipate it and to experience it, the smells and the sights and the sounds of it all, the whole carnival of rock and roll and the circus of movies, it's a beautiful thing, and people don't even have the time to do it anymore. Everything is so quick.

Movie stars used to be Paul Newman, Robert Redford, Jimmy Stewart, Robert Mitchum, and Fredric March. Now movie stars are short little fat kids with curly hair. They're in movies where they go to Mexico and get in trouble with a goat and things like that. That's what a big movie is now.

One night a little more than a year ago, I was sitting around bitching with a buddy of mine down here about how there are not any good movies anymore and how every now and then I have to go out and be in a movie and play some task force leader just to pay the bills. So I go into the office, and I start looking around at these plaques I have in there for writing shit and think, *Well, goddammit, just write your own movie like you used to.* You know, you reach a certain level in your career, and you start thinking it's gotta be done *that* way, but then I realized things are never changed by rich people. If you look back through history, things are changed by poor people. Maybe not necessarily *poor* people, but whoever is on the bottom, and I started thinking, *Instead of being on your high horse, look at it like, well, I'm a little shit with no money and nothing at all, and I gotta start all over, and so if I'm going to make my own thing, I can't say, well, I want $100 million to do it. I gotta do it like I used to do it.* Then I started thinking about what movie I was gonna write.

Now, sometimes you don't have a conscious thought about something, yet it's been there all along burning underneath you. For this album J.D. and I made, I wrote a song called "Jayne Mansfield's Car" about something that always fascinated me about my dad. You know by now I was raised pretty poor in the South and my dad was a hotheaded little Irishman. And as I said, we didn't get along very well—he didn't pay much attention to me, period—but one thing that we did together was, and he was a morbid guy, from the time I was probably four years old, he would take me to see the aftermath of car wrecks. We would go out there, and he would study them. I think he had a fascination with the horror, but at the same time—and he wasn't a very *articulate* guy—I think he wondered about life and death a lot. I think he was fascinated by what the people in the car—who had died—were thinking when it happened, how it happened, whether or not they were scared when they went up the tree, if the accident knocked them out enough to where they didn't feel it. I think he thought about all that stuff and how this poor son-of-a-bitch was just going to get a roll of toilet paper and if he hadn't been, then he'd still be alive. So how does that fit into the scheme of things? Is there a God? Is there a devil? Is there a heaven or a hell? Are we aliens? Somehow I think he had some thought process there.

THERE WASN'T REALLY A LOT OF ENTERTAINMENT IN OUR SMALL TOWN, but the carnival would come around every now and then. Some snake oil salesman figured out a long time ago that people are really fascinated with other people's pain and misery, so they'd bring around the Spider Woman, the five-legged cow, and these other sideshows. It's been going on forever. It's not like human nature changed recently, it's that now there's more outlets for this fascination. Back in the old days, what was there? Before the printing press—which I saw on some show was the number-one invention of all time because it put news out in mass fashion—

they were feeding Christians to lions and watching gladiators chop one another to bits. People have always wanted to see that shit, you know? So all of a sudden in the sixties, maybe even before that, these guys started bringing things around and charging you a dollar to see them because it's like, hey, people like to see this shit, let's make some money off it.

They also brought around car wrecks—Bonnie and Clyde's car with all the bullet holes in it, stuff like that. One time they brought Jayne Mansfield's car around, and my dad of course took me to see it. I was in my early teens by that time. Tom Epperson came out to see it too. So we paid our fifty cents or dollar or whatever it was to walk up on a little stage, and for an extra fifty cents we got to look in this destroyed car. Jayne Mansfield's car. One of the added attractions to this deal was a mannequin head with a wig on it and fake blood on the wig. People think she was decapitated, but she wasn't, she was scalped. There's a technical name for it, I don't know what it is. Tom remembers the head being in the backseat, I remember it being in the front passenger floorboard—who knows who's right?—but anyway, people didn't walk up, look in there, and go, "Aw geez, that's stupid, they got a mannequin head here." They looked at it like they were looking at the Grand Canyon.

Now, there are a couple of ways to look at that. I have friends who are great tourists. Not just tourists, but people who are interested in a bunch of shit.

When I was making *Pushing Tin* in Toronto, a friend of mine who was on the movie said, "Hey, the shoe museum is here," so I went to the shoe museum. Well, I get there, and after I see about ten pairs of shoes—the kind of shoes that Chiang Kai-shek wore, the kind of shoes that they used to bind people's feet in, the shoes that Elizabeth the Third or whatever wore—all I want to do is go outside and have a cigarette, because to me it's all just a pair of shoes. But a lot of people like stuff like that. I don't mind. I really don't want to go to the Nestlé factory and shit like that. But I know people who do. And I'm fascinated with World War II and the Civil War to a degree, so I'll go look at *that* stuff.

So these people go see this car, and as I said, to them it isn't just some mannequin head. It's *her* head on the floorboard, and it starts them thinking how it happened. "Wow! They ran up under this mosquito spray truck, and look, the top is all ripped off, and *oh*! She must have gone out *that* door!"

So I'd always wanted to do something on that. That's why we wrote the song, and I loved that title: "Jayne Mansfield's Car." But it's not a movie about Jayne Mansfield. What *Jayne Mansfield's Car* is actually about is how different generations view war and are affected by it. It's done in a darkly humorous way for the most part, with some drama in there too. It's also about the fascination and the fear of life and death, and how families are affected by the dichotomy. Jayne Mansfield was killed in 1967, and the movie takes place in 1969, so it's around the time of her death, and her car does figure into the movie, but it's really just a metaphor.

I often find that when you can explain what a movie is about, it's usually not very good. If it's about a butler who goes insane and kills everybody and it turns out he was never really the butler, but the father, that's fine, I guess. But *Jayne Mansfield's Car* is a movie that we made in the spirit of the movies that I loved in the fifties, sixties, and seventies, so hopefully the people who loved those movies will go and see this one.

✳

SO NOW A DINOSAUR LIKE ME COMES IN AND SAYS, "HEY, I HAVE A MOVIE I want to make that actually says something, and the cast list is me, Robert Duvall, John Hurt, Kevin Bacon, Ray Stevenson, and all these other people, but I need $11.5 million to make it." Ten years ago they would've shit themselves and opened the checkbook. But now they say, "Well, yeah, but you guys are these real actor guys, and there's going to be a lot of talking in it and stuff. There's no real market for that, so we'll give you $4 million to make it." So when your movie comes out and you've got a boom shot in one wall that you didn't have the money to take out and everybody goes, "See? They make those shitty little art movies and the curly-haired little fat kid's movie didn't have a boom shot in it," well, yeah, no fucking wonder. That's because you gave $75 fucking million to the curly-haired kid to make the most vapid horseshit you've ever seen in your life.

I went around to everybody in town to try to get them to make this movie, and everybody wanted to finance it, but they wanted to finance it for a fraction of what I needed to make it, which wasn't much to begin with. And this is, by the way, with me and the other actors making nothing. We didn't even ask for any money. These are my friends, and they said they'd do it because they wanted to do something decent. Everyone questioned the foreign value. "The Japanese are never going to go out in droves to see this because it's about America." So guess who financed it? Well, not the Japanese, but my manager gets a call from these Russian guys who had read the script and an interview with me saying you can't get a decent movie made anymore, and they say, "We want to finance your movie." So *Jayne Mansfield's Car,* which is about a British family and an American family meeting up in Alabama in 1969 and about their connection to each other through war, is financed by Russians.

We've cut the movie—we have the final cut. We've done the music. We've put together sound effects. We're in the process of getting it all wrapped up. It's going to be ready in about two weeks, and I know I'll be able to sit back, look at this movie, and truly believe we did what we set out to do. If there's something you overlook, you kick yourself in the ass for the rest of your life, but we've taken great care with this one. I feel it emotionally, I feel the humor, it looks right, feels right, the cast was right, I think everybody involved did their job, and I think it's a really, really good movie. We dedicated the movie to Rick Dial, my old buddy who was in *Sling Blade* and *The Apostle* and was *going* to be in *Jayne Mansfield's Car,* but passed away. Rick, God rest his soul, was a guy I grew up with. I put him in *Sling Blade,* and he actually ended up with an acting career, doing twelve or thirteen movies.

AGAIN, I'M NOT ONE OF THESE GUYS WHO SAYS THAT INDEPENDENT films are the only good films. I did a big blockbuster movie, *Armageddon,* and a lot of people say, "*Armageddon,* it was a big, splashy Michael Bay movie." I have to tell you something—I tear up a little bit at the end of that movie every time. I think Jerry Bruckheimer is one of the best producers out here, he's a guy who really cares about his movies, and I think they made a terrific movie out of *Armageddon.* I'm proud to have been in that movie. I think it was good, I think it was made with the right spirit and that it still holds up today. A lot of people love that movie. So I'm not trying to say that all big blockbuster movies are bad. There are as many shitty independent films as there are commercial movies. In my mind, the big commercial movies at one point were so good, there wasn't that separation. And there are also what you might call art films—like the one about a one-legged grapefruit salesman who sleeps with his mother and lives in a closet—that bore the hell out of me and a lot of other people.

It's like this time when I first came to L.A. and a girl who I wanted to get in with wanted me to go to this art show in West Hollywood. She and her brother were both artists. So I went with her and saw these squares of beige carpet that I guessed the paintings were going to be hung on—then I found out that the art show was a bunch of squares of beige carpet. All I could say was, "I don't get it, I'm sorry."

What Tom Epperson and I wrote will be on the screen the way we envisioned it from the script. They say you make three movies. The one you write, the one you shoot, and the one you edit. That's true sometimes. I think in this case, the movie was shot and edited already within the script. Those are the ones that I feel comfortable making. That's why I'm not a good guy to hire as a director if you're looking for a person to do somebody else's stuff, because I'm going to be the wrong guy. I'm the right guy to do *my own* shit. Woody Allen does it, and I respect the fact that he knows what he wants to do and he goes and does it. You'll be happy with your shit sometimes, and sometimes you won't, but I guarantee you're the best guy for the job.

CHAPTER FORTY-EIGHT

High Definition in a Cracker Box

The titles changed, the credits changed, and the marquee is
dark
The creature tore the Ritz down, now he owns the block
Twelve bucks'll get you a ticket, for ten bucks you can park
And see high definition in a cracker box

—"Saturday Afternoon a Half Century On"

(Thornton/Andrew)

THE PRODUCERS WILL GET A DISTRIBUTOR HERE WHO I'M GUESSING will then try to get us to cut it from two hours and ten minutes to forty-seven minutes so they can get it into theaters for more showings. These distributors also think they know what they're doing in terms of marketing, but it's like this: let's say you got Mel Tormé, and he makes a new record because somebody said, "Mel, these new songs, they're fantastic. They're like the old days, they're amazing. So let's put it out. But let's put it in an album jacket where you're wearing some big baggy shorts, flashing gang signs, and wearing a cap on sideways so we can sell it to the young people." What happens is, the young people go buy it and they say, "What the fuck is this shit? What are these old-guy songs? I thought he was hip." And then the people who like Mel Tormé see the album cover with his cap on sideways and go, "I'm not buying this Mel Tormé record, Jesus Christ, look at him, he looks like a gangbanger." The next thing you know, nobody buys it.

So, believe me, when the producers get ready to go here and they start looking for the distributor, the distributor is going to say, "Well, it's a little long," and we're going to say, "What difference does that make? *Giant* had a fucking intermission."

Here's the difference between *now* and *then*. We went to the movie theater on Sunday, and they had a double feature, and you got in for thirty cents. We couldn't wait to get to the theater to see movies, and when we could, we would stay all day. Now they can't wait to get out of the theaters. People watch part of a movie on their phone and get sick of it and go do something else. When, or if, they finally finish watching a movie, the first thing they do is get on the Internet and tell everyone how much they hated it. Unless it's about a video game or an angst-ridden teenage vampire.

CHAPTER FORTY-NINE

Let's Go See Movies Again

If you really want to live
There's something you should know
It's a simple secret
Buried not that long ago
You may have to use your voice
And possibly your mind
It may not make sense at first
But leave your screens behind
There's a different kind of integration
And different sights and sounds and touch
And even imagination

—"Look Up" (Thornton/Andrew)

I'M NOT GOING TO BE HEARTBROKEN IF *JAYNE MANSFIELD'S CAR* doesn't become the movie of the year and win the Academy Award. There was a time when I thought about stuff like that, but I don't think about it anymore. I trust that a certain section of the audience will go see it, but the problem is that people don't want to go out to the movie theater anymore. What needs to happen is that we've got to get people who are sitting on their asses watching *Attack of Spartacus* or whatever the hell that show is off their asses and get them to go out to see movies again. People have gotten complacent. They're sitting at home and watching TV because, "Oh, it's twelve dollars now, and I got to buy popcorn," but that's the point of everything I'm saying.

I don't believe in watching movies on a telephone, and I think people ought to get in their damn car and drive to the theater and pay twelve dollars. You pay twelve dollars to get coronary artery disease, so why don't you pay twelve dollars to see a good movie? A pork chop in a restaurant is twenty-four dollars. Go buy a pork chop, cook it yourself, and then go pay twelve bucks to see a movie.

The magic in life is disappearing very quickly, and we've got to get it back. Part of getting it back is getting people who lived in the time when there actually *was* magical stuff to participate again, because if we don't, it'll completely disappear. *So let's go out to the theater.* Guys my age get these gadgets, and they say, "Look, I just got this thing, it's the size of a thimble, and I can watch a movie, listen to music, read a book, and it can jack you off! All I got to do is take this fucking thing, push a little button, and I don't have to do anything ever again!"

I WATCH MOVIES FOR ENTERTAINMENT, TOO, AND LIKE ANYBODY ELSE, I don't only like good stuff. I like horrible shit sometimes. I've seen horrible movies that made me cry like a baby. I've seen movies most people wouldn't find funny that made me laugh because something in it struck a chord from my childhood.

I've talked a lot about things I hate, and I do hate a lot, but it's not because of the thing itself—it's because of the people who are making the thing. If somebody gives something their all and loves what they're doing, God bless them. Do it. Follow your dream. Do what you love. But nowadays, there are so many people out there who thrive on hating things *just* for the sake of hating. They think that hating something and talking bad about things make them seem more cool or hip. I can boil down my point of view to this: I'm against people who are against shit. I don't care who you are, if you *believe* in what you're doing, I'm all for you. But believe in whatever it is you believe in with all your heart and soul.

CHAPTER FIFTY

Billy the Dad

You showed me what an echo looks like dancin' in the shade
And how the snails get dressed up when they go out on
parade
You've painted me a rainbow on the inside of my eye
So I can see it anytime in the blueberry sky

—"Blueberry Sky" (Thornton/Andrew)

THIS JUNE, HARRY WILL BE EIGHTEEN AND WILLIE WILL BE NINETEEN, which boggles my mind. Willie: piercings, tattoos, long hair, hanging out with his friends playing video games and still going to the mall, like a California rock-and-roll kid. He plays bass in a band that plays I don't know what type of music, and every time I tell somebody what Willie plays in front of him, he says, "No, Dad, don't be an idiot, it's not called that, it's called (whatever else)."

Then my other son, who never talked to me much about what he did in school—he's very quiet—just graduated from the Explorer Program for the L.A. County Sheriff's Association and wants to join the Marines and then become a deputy sheriff. I think the only reason he wants to do it is so he can arrest his brother someday. I'm pretty convinced of that.

I never saw that coming with Harry. This shy, quiet kid who just had a little skateboard shop in his house, working on his skateboards and shooting basketball, and all of a sudden here he is, all buff with a drill instructor.

And then there's little Bella, who belongs to me and Connie. In this house it's me, Connie, Bella, and Willie. It's funny having a seven-year-old daughter and an eighteen-year-old son living in the same house.

Bella wants to be a paleontologist, and whatever you call a butterfly-ologist. She raises caterpillars to butterflies, and they become chrysalises and fly around the yard, then come back and make more butterflies. We're always buying milkweed plants for them. She knows so much about animals. She's friends with Dr. Scott Sampson, the paleontologist who does *Dinosaur Train*. That's my seven-year-old's friend.

When we were making *Jayne Mansfield's Car,* Duvall wanted to know what we were doing one day. He wanted me to go eat meat with him or whatever because he's obsessed with meat. I said we were going to a botanical garden, where they have an endangered-frog thing where they'll take us behind the scenes. So Duvall and Luciana, his wife, actually ended up going with us to this thing, along with my old buddy Barry Markowitz, my cinematographer. Bella takes them into this frog thing, and I guess they thought they were going to go into this little frog display and Bella was going to say, "Looky, Mommy, look at the frog!" She gave Duvall and Barry a lesson on amphibians that you can't imagine. She won't watch cartoons, except for *Dinosaur Train,* because it has real stuff in it too and it's educational. She'll only watch educational programming. She watches this series that Oprah Winfrey does, *Life,* and she watches *Planet Earth.* I've learned more about science through my seven-year-old in the last few years than I ever learned in my entire miserable career in school. This beautiful little seven-year-old is the center of my day, every day, because Willie is off with his pals doing stuff. The boys and Connie take center stage at night when Bella is asleep.

I'm proud of these kids. They're amazing in their own very, very different ways. They really change your life, and you never stop worrying again, believe me, because you never know what road it might go down. I am trying my best as their dad, but I believe these kids are going to be okay because I'm also their friend. But not on Facebook.

> *I hope you'll forgive me if I talk too much*
> *But it's been bottled up inside*
> *You see a little part of me is out of touch*
> *Since a pretty big part of me died*
> *To tell you the truth, I'm kinda glad you're here*
> *Soaked to the bone or not*
> *At the moment it seems to be pretty clear*
> *We're the only friends we got*
> —From "Dead End Drive"

Acknowledgments

First of all I'd like to thank my family for all their patience and support: my mother, Virginia; my brother John and his family Jennifer, James, and Ginny; the kids, Willie and Bella and Harry; the boys' mom Pietra and a host of aunts, uncles, nieces, nephews, and cousins; my brother Jimmy; my dad and my grandparents, God rest their souls. To my love Connie and her family; Big and Little Walter, Aggie, Maya, Chris, Beatrice and Kragen, Carrie, Peter, and Chloe. Without my family I wouldn't even be able to face breakfast.

Also special thanks to Kinky and all his pals who sat around and listened to me ramble: Daniel Taub, Ted Mann, John Mankiewicz, Twink Caplan, Larry "Ratso" Sloman, Louie Kemp, Mike Simmons, and Danny Hutton.

From William Morrow Books: Liate Stehlik, Lynn Grady, Shelby Meizlik, Tavia Kowalchuk, Shawn Nicholls, Joyce Wong, Mary Schuck, and Susan Amster.

From Vigliano and Associates: David Vigliano, Olga Vezeris, Matthew Carlini, and Anthony Mattero.

To Sage Ferrero for all her hard work and to Dylan for loaning her out. To Amélie Frank and all the Planeteers. You keep me stumbling along.

To my coworkers over the years in the movie world: Kristin

Scott Irving, Bruce Heller, Oren Segal, Felicia Molinari, Lynne Eagan, Joani Yarbrough, Mr. P, Keith Sayer, Arnold Robinson, Paul Bloch, Geyer Kosinski, Jerry Myman, Bob Myman, Barry Markowitz, Doug Hall, Jim Hensz, Chis Halle, Susan Strubel, Annie Miller, Wendy Chuck, Karen Patch, Julie Weiss, Dwayne Grady, Clark Hunter, Paul Ledford, Harve Cook, Kenny Roth, Steve Search, Bob Salerno, Larry Meistrich, Dave Bushell, Brandon Rosser, Buddy Van Horn, and many others.

In the music world: My pal and cofounder of the Boxmasters J. D. Andrew, original member Mike Butler and current Boxmaster and longtime music partner Brad Davis, and their families.

All the road members of the solo tours and Boxmaster tours over the years: Mike Bruce, Teddy Andreadis, Danny Baker, Larry Byrd, Chuck Garric, Mike Shipp, Jody Maphis, Jon Rauhouse, Marty Rifkin, Roger "Tiny" Kohrs, Daryl Johnson, Matt Laug, Eric Singer, Damon Johnson, Eric Dover, Ryan Roxy, Gregg Stocki, Steve Arnold, Mike Finnigan, Mica Roberts, Randy Mitchell, Stephen Bruton, and others probably and all their families.

To the road and studio crews over the years: Jim Mitchell, Dirty Don, Micro, Bobby O.D., Dan Druff, Raz, Raymond Hardy, Terry Wieland, Tom Mayhue, McBob, Hoover, Jamo, Sack, Steve Winstead, bus drivers Chuck & Shaggy.

What follows is a list of friends, coworkers, influences (some I've known, some I haven't) in music, movies, and just life. Basically people who just plain old don't suck. I will leave people out because I'm not that bright and I'm in a rush. Also, this is for the people I'm thanking so stuff the comments about how long it is and put the fucking book down. I wouldn't have shit if I didn't have the people in these acknowledgments. They're the people that make up the journey:

Coby Leed, Katja Biesanz, Dan Di Vito, Esperanza and family and Jessica and family, the Zappas, Tommy & Jeanne Shaw, J. P. Shellnutt, Ritchie Montgomery, Brent Briscoe, Greg Littman and family, Forrest Witt, Jesse Dabson, Ric Krause, Tom Challis, Joe Coppolletta, Don Blakely, Barnaby Hazen, Phil Walden, Alan Walden, JY, James Haven, Marcheline Bertrand, Holly Goline, Jim and Helene Ladd, Mark and Brian, Ernest Borgnine, Bo Hopkins, Roger Harrison, Fred Roos, Jim Jacks, Jim Varney, Ben Myron, Emily Schweber, Thomas Jane, Jeff Bridges, Nitty Gritty Dirt Band guys, Diana Walker, Rod, Klaus, Nancy, Peter, Scott and everyone at the Sunset Marquis, Faryal Russell, Donnie Fritts, Terry and Anita Pace, The Muscle Shoals Gang, Jerry Lee Lewis, Jim Dandy, Rickie Lee, and Black Oak Arkansas, Levon Helm, Slash, Alice Cooper, Dewey Bunnell, Gerry Beckley, Michael Nesmith, Mickey Dolenz, Peter Tork, Davy Jones, The Allman Brothers, Bob Teitel, George Tillman, Natalie Canerday, Mary Cross, Sarah Tackett, Barry Battles, Griffin Hood, Chuck Leavell, Billy Gibbons, Dusty Hill, Frank Beard, Pablo Gamboa and the whole ZZ Top world, Scott Weiss, Rick and all the Dial family, all my Malvern H.S. pals, Rick Calhoun, The Yardleys, Tom Epperson and Stefanie Ames, the Carter-Cash Family, the Scruggs Family, Prophet Omega, Horton Foote, Doug Jackson, Marty Stuart, Connie Smith, Porter Wagoner, Kris Kristofferson and family, Willie Nelson and family, Waylon Jennings, Shooter Jennings, Jessi Colter, Matt Sorum, Sharon Corbitt, Joe Ely, Ray Benson, Billy Joe Shaver, Nick Shipp, Kenny Hall, Harry Dean Stanton, Lee Sklar, Warren and Steph Haynes, Warren Zevon, Jorge Calderon, Graham Nash, Joe Walsh, Steve Lukather, Leah Haynes, Jed Leiber, Jeff Barry, John Kay, Keith Allison, Jimmy Johnson, David Spero, Brook Simons, Dave Warden, Owen Wilson, Luke Wilson,

Woody Harrelson, Frank Wuliger, Dan Shurwin, Paul Revere, John Prine, Brad Wilson, Steven Vail, John Widlock, Rob Carliner, Frank Bacchus, Jennifer and the Teatro Gang, Mark Howard, Joe McCracken, Brian Blade, Brady Blade, Joe Murdock, James Pierce, Burl White, Danny Turner, Brian Wingo, Rex, Tim Ross, the guys in Cottonwood, Brown, Hoochie, Eric, Steve and Mark, Vic Chesnutt, Mickey Jones, Tom Waits, Colonel Bruce Hampton, Michael Buffalo Smith, The Big G, Will and Sandrine Lee, David Adelson, David Wild. Geoff Emerick, Alan Parsons, Jewel, Howard Kaylan, The Ventures, The Petocz's, Robbie Clyne, Rickey Medlocke and all the Skynyrd guys, Manuel, Phil Donahue, Marlo Thomas, Tony Thomas and St. Judes. My pals from Henderson State University.

John Calley, Bruce Dern, Bruce Willis, Barry Levinson, Cate Blanchett, Mike Newell, Dennis Quaid, John Hurt, Kevin Bacon, Katherine LaNasa, Robert Duvall, Ray Stevenson, Robert Patrick, Frances O'Connor, Shawnee Smith, Marshall Allman, John Patrick Amedori, Ron White and Margo Rey, Michael Blakey, Drew Edwards, Lucy Sabini, Bill Cummisky, John DeChristopher, Ryan Smith, Evan O'Brien, Kim Graham, Tippi Hedren, Irma P. Hall, Sam Raimi, John Lee Hancock, Andy Griffith, Don Knotts, George Lindsay, Merle Haggard, George Jones, Alan & Debra Jenkins, Victoria Pearman, Becca and Bonnie Bramlett, Margarette Marissen, Joel Coen, Ethan Coen, Fran McDormand, John Curtis, Carl Franklin, Jessie Beaton, Roger Ebert and Charlie "Chaz" Hammel-Smith, Gene and Marlene Siskel, Leonard Maltin and Alice Tlusty, Peter Bogdanovich, John Cusack, Harold Ramis, Matty Simmons and everyone at *National Lampoon*, Heath Ledger, Mitch Glazer and Kelly Lynch, Jeffrey Lyons, Tony La Russa, Yadier Molina, Bobby Knight, John Loar, Kevin Pollack, Jim Leyland, Bob Gibson, Brooks

Robinson, Stan Musial, Marty Henden, Aggie Ceriotti, The Cardinals period, Stanley Kramer and the Kramer family, Phil Walden, Charles Nelson Reilly, Charlie Rose, Ann Curry, Lara Shriftman, Lara Spencer, Richard Harris, Alec Guinness, Taylor Hackford, Martin Landau and family, Ed Solomon, Kurt Russell, Burl Ives, Dani Jansen, Don Rickles, Michael Keaton, James Caan, Marlon Brando, Phil, Brent and Roy D. Mercer, Tracy Kirshbaum, the Clintons, Poodie Locke, Joe Buck, Jack Buck, Richard Perry, Jane Fonda, Troy Garity, Penélope Cruz, Lauren Graham, Debbie Carrington, Brett Kelley, Jason Patric, Patrick Wilson, Bridget Fonda, Julio Mechoso, Keisha Kalfin, Ruben Blades, Henry Thomas, Lucas Black, Jimmy Hampton, Carol Doran, Peter Tilden, Rick Linklater, Alli Shearmur, Janet Yang, Carlos Castaneda, Steven Vail, Jeff Lester, Susan Anton, Bill Paxton, Tom Hanks, Jeffrey Katzenberg, Brian Grazer, Rick Overton, Jay Roach, Sally Menke, Joan Sobel, Dean Parisot, Fred Raskin, Ron Howard, Terry Zwigoff, Lauren Zuckerman, Sergei Bespalov, Alexander Rodnyansky, Ivan Phillipov, Jim Brubaker, Janet Waddles, Gina Warendorp, the cast and crews of all the movies I've ever done, Morgan Freeman, Roddy McDowall, Gregory Peck, Elizabeth Taylor, Clint Eastwood, Jack Nicholson, Sean Penn, Julia Roberts, Eric Roberts, Eliza Simons, Gary Busey, Nick Nolte, Powers Booth, Dr. Richard Dwyer, the Arquettes, Mary Cross, Sandra Lucchessi, Ro Diamond, Susie Schwartz, Mary Vernieu, Janet Hirshenson, Jane Jenkins, Cathy Henderson, Barbara Hanley, Fran Bascom, Jerry Bruckheimer, Martin Scorsese, Frederic March, Peter Sellers, Montgomery Clift, John Ritter, Amy Yasbeck, Harry Thomason, Linda Bloodworth-Thomason, Burt Reynolds, Hal Holbrook, Charles Durning, Ronnie Yeskel, Liz Larner, Beth McGroarty, Brad Pitt, George Clooney, Seth McFarlane and his gang for producing a brilliant world, and Stephen King, and now it's getting stupid and I've left so many people out but for shit's sake.

Special thanks to my great friends who said words that are too kind. I am humbled. Angelina Jolie, Tom Epperson, Robert Duvall, Dwight Yoakam, Daniel Lanois. And to Adam Korn and Trish Daly and everyone at William Morrow and HarperCollins. And sports, music, movies, Austin, Texas; Memphis, Tennessee; and New Orleans, Louisiana; and everyone who has the balls to try to keep swimming up shit creek.

Sometimes I see shapes in the air
Sometimes I see the faces that they wear
Maybe they're old friends who don't
mean any harm
Could be the chill I feel is
meant to keep me warm
as I man my lonely Post
in this Cave Full of Ghosts

Sleep won't ~~come~~ seem to come
but exhaustion never goes
my ~~conciousness~~ is haunted
By dreams that never ~~show~~
~~Just just because I never let~~
~~them ~~
~~The past is here with me~~
~~It's the only~~
The ~~only~~ way I ~~know to~~ live
~~is killing~~ everyone
my way of life grew ~~up and moved~~ right
~~out of~~ ~~town~~
and ~~left~~ a ~~still~~ Body no one ever found